# IT'S ~~MY~~ YOUR DREAM

## Eight Elements to Guide
## Your Business Success

# Gregory K. McAfee

ISBN-10: 1570740135
ISBN-13: 978-1-57074-013-8


Printed in the United States of America

Printed by:
Greyden Press, LLC
2251 Arbor Boulevard
Dayton, OH 45439
www.greydenpress.com

*Advance Praise for*

## It's ~~My~~ Your Dream
### by
### Gregory K. McAfee

"In his book, *It's ~~My~~ Your Dream*, HVAC Contractor and Author Greg McAfee provides a concise look into the thinking, commitment, and effort it takes to set and operate a successful HVAC contracting firm in the twenty-first century. His down-to-earth writing style is easy to relate to as he tells the tale of how he found himself changing his youthful dreams into a new reality that is the basis of his life's work. Step by step, he lays out the path to success, providing tips on what is necessary, and spinning anecdotal tales that highlight the faux pas he made and how to avoid them. Whether you're thinking about getting into the HVAC business or are just looking for some plain old advice, this book is an excellent choice. Congratulations to Greg McAfee and all the people who have helped his company to be a success."

Michael S. Weil
Editorial Director
*Contracting Business.com* magazine
*HPAC Engineering Magazine*
HVAC-Talk.com

"If you own a business or if you want to own a business, I recommend **It's ~~My~~ Your Dream.** Greg McAfee's eight rules for success are elegantly simple, yet profound, and are built from his entrepreneurial experiences. This book is full of practical, well-considered advice. Buy it and read it. You'll be glad you did."

David Heimer
Chief Operating Officer
Service Roundtable

## Acknowledgments

I want to first thank God for all the blessings and opportunities He's given me so far in this life.

Thanks to my Mom and Dad for giving me life and responsibilities and for disciplining me when I needed it.

Thanks to my wife Naomi for loving me even when I wasn't lovable. Thanks, Naomi, for your support and prayers over the years.

To my two kids, Travis and Tiffany, I'm glad you were born! Never forget that with God, all things are possible.

To my Leadership Team, thanks for working with me and catching my dream. It couldn't happen without you!

Thanks to the entire McAfee team for all your hard work, making sure we take care of our customers, and for representing my name well! A special thanks to Kevin Turner for managing the field duties. It's relieved me of much responsibility so I can dream.

Thanks to the McAfee Board of Advisors, Anita W., Michael K., and Steve L., for all your help over the past few years.

Thanks to Tracy Staley for helping me write this book and to Angie Downey for proofing, rewriting, and reading it over many times.

Thanks to Autumn Conley, Book Editor, autiej@gmail.com, for performing the final editing and providing the resources.

# Table of Contents

## Preface

I thought it was my dream to work at Firestone Tire and Rubber Company.

I was born in Akron, Ohio and grew up in the small industrial town of Mansfield in the late sixties and seventies. I watched my father and grandfather build long careers in the tire factory and on the warehouse floors; they had security, as well as an identity. They rarely missed work, and they both came home reeking of rubber. In spite of the fact that most would find it a nearly intolerable stench, it was the norm to hear my grandmother proclaim, "I love that smell!" when my grandfather came in the door. "It puts the bread and butter on the table," she gratefully declared.

I was primed to follow in their footsteps, but working at Firestone turned out to be a world away from the dream I would eventually pursue. In 1990, I followed that dream and launched McAfee Heating and Air Conditioning Company, Inc. Since then, I've worked to build a company rooted in quality service and ethical business practices. Along the way, I have developed a passion for helping other entrepreneurs follow their own dreams. Many companies fail in their early years, but dreams should not stop there.

As I have studied how McAfee has blossomed from its roots to an award-winning, successful small business, I have realized the eight principles that have guided the growth: be strategic; be teachable; be a coach; be known; be giving; be innovative; be passionate; and be ready.

Through the next eight chapters, we'll walk through each of these principles, with examples from my business as well as some from other entrepreneurs who have also followed their dreams.

## From Firestone to Entrepreneur

I spent my childhood working odd jobs: delivering papers, selling vegetables door to door, and picking apples. I worked two jobs in high school, and I loved working, even though school bored me to the point where I absolutely couldn't wait to get out. Due to my distaste for all things academic, I graduated with a low GPA. At 19, when a job opened at a new Firestone facility in Dayton, Ohio, I loaded my pickup truck with a bed, a chair, and the few other things I could call my own and followed my Firestone dream.

I wasn't familiar with Dayton at the time, but I jumped at the opportunity to move. It was the early 1980s, and industrial life was thriving. As a third-generation Firestone employee, I was excited about and appreciative of the opportunity.

Like my dad, I arrived almost every morning well before the six thirty a.m. starting time. I drove a forklift and entertained myself by trying to see how fast I could work and how many pounds of tires I could load in a day. Unfortunately, this was not an acceptable concept in a unionized workplace. Working hard and fast was not the best way to win friends (imagine that!), but I worked hard and fast anyway. For a short time, I even had the warehouse manager posting goals and records on a bulletin board.

This wasn't the norm and didn't sit well with the other workers, so the idea fizzled out. What a shame! Truly, as the old proverb goes, "where there is no vision, the people perish." Each day around one p.m. the department supervisor came around offering overtime, and I rarely turned it down. I was — and still am — grateful for the opportunity to work at Firestone.

About three years into the job, I glimpsed at a much older forklift driver moving tires around the warehouse. As I watched him toil, something dawned on me: I didn't want to spend my life doing that. As much as I thought I was living my dream, I knew I didn't want that man to be me thirty years later. *Something new and different has to be out there,* I told myself. *I just need to find it.*

I found it in the United States Marine Corps. In high school, a good friend had tried to get me to join under the Marines Buddy Enlistment Program. While it was only a lingering idea at first, I decided that my best option to get me off that forklift was to become one of the few and the proud. I enlisted in 1986, attended boot camp at Parris Island and was stationed at Twentynine Palms, California. Later, back in Dayton, when I was again working full time at Firestone, I served in the Reserves on weekends.

The Marines equipped me well for business, and during my enlistment, I learned many traits that have helped me along the way, such as how to be more disciplined, structured, and confident. I also took a class in refrigeration, recalling my dad's sage advice that I should someday go into heating, ventilating, and air conditioning (HVAC). "There will always be work," he said, and I never forgot that. After my service in the Marines, I enrolled in classes at the county vocational school. By that time, my father was also working for Firestone in Dayton, and he took the class with me. In that class, a seed was planted, and my dream began to change.

No longer did I want to work at Firestone for the rest of my life. As I sat

in those classes, I decided that someday, I would own my own business.

Even though I didn't know how or when it would all happen, the dream

became very clear to me.

I daydreamed about it as I worked days at Firestone (there's a lot

of time for thinking when you're rather mindlessly driving a forklift

around). As I dreamed of owning my own business and continued the

HVAC classes, I had business cards made: my name on one side and

Dad's on the other.

My instructor urged me to get some hands-on experience before

launching out on my own. I gladly heeded his advice and took a leap of

faith. I left my job at Firestone after being hired on as a helper at a small

HVAC company in a Dayton suburb, and this came with a substantial pay

cut: a risk I encourage you to take if it gets you closer to your dream.

Being willing to work for less pay can — believe it or not — bring you

greater gains in your career. Little did I know that a pay reduction would

reap such big dividends later. I worked for that little company for nine

months before the owner decided I should be laid off. In an attempt to

soften the blow, he said, "You'll never make it as a mechanic." I was devastated and embarrassed, but in the end, he was right. Besides, you haven't really lived until you've been fired a few times. The nine months there paid off, though, because I learned a lot of what not to do in business.

After my "layoff," I took another job with an HVAC company, where I started as a service technician. During my stay there, I discovered that I had a knack for selling; many times, I outsold their full-time salesman. I continued to work there while big changes came in my personal life: namely, marrying my wife Naomi and purchasing our first home. Then, I was let go again. Six months later, that company closed its doors.

Naomi had a full-time job that paid most of our bills, so even though I had hoped to stay on there to bolster my experience, we decided as a couple that it was as good a time as any to take the chance and launch my own business. It was time to give that dream of mine some real wings, and I hoped it could fly!

* * *

I did not have a huge nest-egg to help me start my own business. In fact, all I really had was the meager $274 in my bank account and a used Ford Ranger (ironically, one without A/C). In spite of the lack of any substantial capital investment, I took the leap and opened McAfee

Heating and Air Conditioning Co., Inc.

It was a very slow process, and I've never been a man of great patience. It was a yet another learning opportunity for me, however, for what I discovered is that slow growth pays off. I spent days combing through a crisscross directory phone book (something today's entrepreneurs would more quickly and easily do on the Internet). I went street to street, door to door, and made phone calls to pitch my services. It was not easy, for it often took a few hundred meetings and phone calls before I would get one "yes," agreeing to let me perform a service call or system tune-up. Whenever new businesses opened in my area, I drove the trusty old Ford door to door, asked to speak with the managers of the fledgling establishment, and posed one simple question: "Have you had your heating and air system serviced lately?" This often led to more work, and I did that work out of our home, a 900-square-foot ranch home in Beavercreek, a suburb of Dayton.

The days were long and a little lonely; I recall one particularly worrisome time when the phone didn't ring for two weeks. However, I kept driving my truck around, with the McAfee logo plastered on the side. Around that time, someone said to me, "I see your trucks everywhere!"

and I knew I was making progress since I only had one truck. My truck

had a service cap and ladder on top so that I could do jobs right away, but

often I chose to schedule appointments to return to do the work, assuming

that if I seemed busier than I actually was, clients would have more

confidence in my work. Perception is everything! The busiest restaurants

get the most business, right? If everyone is eating there, it must be good.

Eventually, I got a nice break with a contract to service home

warranty clients. This put me right in people's driveways, doing ten to

fifteen service calls a week. Although I only stayed with the home

warranty business for a year, it made a significant impact and helped me

get started. Today, I advise new companies to try the home warranty

business, but I urge you not to stop there. If you are an entrepreneur in any

field, you must know when to pull the plug and rely on yourself, and that

time had come for me. It was time to make the leap into being a viable

business.

* * *

When my business was in its infancy, we did a few critical things

right. We set ourselves up as a professional business from the start. My

sister-in-law, Northa S., is a diligent bookkeeper, and she made sure we

logged our expenses, recorded all income, and paid our taxes.

Because of her, I learned to enjoy reviewing monthly reports. Whether out of disorganization or deception, businesses that try to skimp on accounting eventually suffer for it. Get your books in order and pay your taxes from the start. You'll be glad you did and probably won't be around long if you don't.

Second, I did some work for an accountant, who gave me the wise advice of paying myself a set salary. Up to that point, for my first year of business, I hadn't paid myself at all other than occasionally withdrawal of fifty bucks here and there. This accountant suggested I begin paying myself right away and not waver from it. We didn't think we could afford it, but I started paying myself $1,200 monthly and increased it gradually every six months. As it turned out, his advice was good counsel, and I haven't missed a paycheck since.

We also purposely avoided debt. I doubt we would be in business today if I had taken on a large credit load in the early years. Aside from a few short lines of credit that we paid off quickly, we only purchased what we could afford. In fact, I didn't even take our first line of credit for nine years. By keeping our debt low (both then and now), I have been able to rest well at night. From savings, we were able to construct our first building, a twenty-four-by-twenty-four-foot garage, and we did that debt free. We used half of the facility as our office and the other half as a warehouse. We were thrilled to have a space to work outside of my home, but it wasn't easy. We had no plumbing in the garage, so when we finally hired an office employee, she had to walk to our house to use the restroom, and the rest of our team had to make pit stops elsewhere when they were out in the field.

It wasn't only plumbing that we lacked, but privacy. Whenever I had to have a serious meeting with a team member, everyone had to leave the office so we could talk in private. In spite of our one-room office and our lack of indoor plumbing, we somehow managed to do almost one million dollars in sales right out of that little garage.

**Make Sure Your Dream Fits Your Family**

Does your dream fit your family? If it doesn't, there's nothing but trouble ahead for you, your spouse, your children, and your business. Sit down with your spouse as you set goals for your new venture. Dream together. Find common ground when it comes to how much time you will commit to the business during the startup phase. Discuss how this endeavor will impact your family. Will your spouse shoulder more of the household and family responsibilities? How do you both feel about debt?

> Does s/he want to work with you? Where do you both
> want to be in five, ten, or twenty years? As your business
> grows and changes, it's wise to revisit and talk through
> these issues often. Making these tough discussions initially
> can save pain and heartache later–both personally and
> professionally.

Today, when I consult other companies, the owners often ask,

"How long will it take for my business to really take off?" This is really

difficult to say. For us, the eighth year of business was a turning point. A

lack of space kept us from adding more sales and office staff. So, in 1996,

we bought a three-acre tract in a business area of Kettering, Ohio. One

year later, with the land paid off, we built an 11,000-square-foot building.

We thought the building would be more affordable if we leased a portion

of it to another business; however, to our surprise — or I should say

shock? — the space sat vacant for eighteen months.

So, that mortgage payment stayed at the top of our prayer list, and

it was a struggle to pay it. We survived, but the stress of such

overwhelming debt reinforced why debt hadn't been part of our culture in

the first place.

Much of our personal business philosophy was born out of the first business book I read, *Business by the Book*, by Larry Burkett, the Dave Ramsey of the 1980s. From then till now, his financial guidance has helped many Christian businessmen and women build their enterprises upon Biblical principles. He advocates keeping debt low, paying your suppliers and employees before paying yourself, and remembering that a good name is worth more than great riches. I clung to those teachings in the beginning, and I still adhere to them today. Why? Because they have worked well for me and have proven true time and time again.

That said, as with every business, we did undergo some trial and error, and we didn't do everything right in the early days. For one thing, I made some hiring mistakes: Imagine finding out that an employee you just sent on a call either wasn't insurable or had a criminal record! I also took on a few business lines that did not fit our company well and held on to them for too long. I attempted to do many of the daily tasks of running the business, including some I clearly wasn't qualified to do. While I kept my debt low, that also meant I didn't establish enough credit for when I needed it. We were certainly more *re*active than *pro*active in those days, which hurt us in the slower months. We waited too long to invest in a computerized scheduling system, and we relied on an old-fashioned appointment book for the first twelve years of business. "Who's got the book?" was a regular call around the office.

Thankfully, though, we were able to avoid any catastrophic mistakes. According to the U.S. Department of Commerce, more than one million new businesses are started in this country annually, and nearly 50 percent fail in the first year. After five years, only about 20 percent of the companies remain in business. Within ten years, only 5 percent are still in business. New companies spend much of their energy just on surviving, but we chose to thrive. How? Keep reading, my friend, and I'll share what I've learned.

* * *

The world has changed dramatically since my father and grandfather were able to build a good, middle-class life on the factory floor, or even since I was running a forklift at Firestone. Although industrial life in America has all but faded, the American dream of running a successful business is still alive and well. If it worked for me, it can work for you. Now, let's find out how...

**Chapter One**

**Be Strategic**

"What do you want to achieve or avoid? The answers to this question are
**objectives**. How will you go about achieving your desire results? The
answer to this you can call **strategy**."

~ William E. Rothschild

Children are prolific dreamers. They are driven by curiosity,
imagination, and boundlessness. If you ask any five-year-old what he
wants to be when he grows up, you can expect a variety of big-dream
answers: astronaut, policeman, fireman, doctor, professional sports hero,
or NASCAR driver, just to name a few. A child's mind races with lofty
notions, backed by hope and goals that grownups dismiss as naïve or
childish.

Unfortunately, for most of us, the dreaming spirit fades as we age
and take on more responsibilities of life. We fear failure and rejection, and
we become impatient. Sometimes we don't even know what our dreams
are. Most often, we don't spend the time it takes to figure out how to take
a dream and plant it so it can grow into reality.

As the American educator and minister Benjamin Mays said, "The tragedy in life doesn't lie in not reaching your goal. The tragedy lies in having no goal to reach." When I started McAfee Heating and Air, my dream was simple: to work for myself. With time, though, my dreams grew and changed. I dreamed of building a garage to work from and then later moving out of that garage into a professional building. I still haven't stopped dreaming; today, I dream of cementing a leading and lasting company with a reputation and legacy my family and employees can be proud to call their own.

Every dream — no matter how small or audacious — must be backed by strategy, or it simply will not take flight. Being strategic has been the key factor in the growth of McAfee Heating and Air. As we have grown, we have become more strategic in the way we operate. Year after year, we refine our goals and get better at pursuing them.

Turning a dream into a reality requires many things. It takes time and a place to dream. It requires the hard work of developing a roadmap. And perhaps most crucial, it requires the perseverance to stay focused and headed in the right direction of the goals you set.

**Finding Time to Dream**

To pursue your dream, you must set aside time to think. Most people pack their days so full that there is little time left — if any — to meditate on their businesses or their lives. Thomas Edison said, "There is no expedient to which a man will not go to avoid the labor of thinking."

Every few weeks, I spend a morning alone in the "Dream Room," my favorite spot at Aileron, an entrepreneur retreat near my home. I take my Leadership Bible and a pad of paper and nothing else; I want nothing else there that could distract me from my thoughts — no phone and no worries. The room has three large glass walls that overlook God's creation, and deer, wild turkeys, and other wildlife roam freely and peacefully near the pond and trees. I go there for the peace and quiet and to take time to really think about my business and life, asking myself important questions like *Where are we going?* and *How do we get there?* Business is founded on thought. Determination and enthusiasm are valuable, but thinking and dreaming are what keep the wheels turning.

I always leave the Dream Room with all the fodder I need for the nitty-gritty planning that comes with setting goals and mapping out the path to meeting them.

**Mapping Your Strategy**

What is strategic planning? It starts with knowing your company: the strengths, weaknesses, opportunities, and threats. It also reflects an understanding of the environment in which you compete: your customers, suppliers, competitors, and market trends. Once you know who you are and where you are, then you can start planning where you are going. This is a vital leadership tool that will boldly direct your company toward reaching the leader's vision. In one word, it's a "process."

I operated McAfee for seven years without a strategic plan, and even after we created one, I didn't know how to use it properly. Some of the mistakes we made — like acquiring a dead-end chimney-cleaning business — might have been avoided if we had weighed those decisions against the goals of our strategic plan. A strategic plan can be as easy as setting goals and then figuring out how and when you can reach them.

Once you have created a vision for your company and where you see yourself in one, five, and ten years from now, the next step is to create a plan for getting there: decide how many people it will require, how much money will be needed, and the resources required to get you there.

Nowadays, we revisit our strategic plan annually. This yearly realignment helps us avoid both minor and serious missteps, all while keeping me on track with my dream.

---

### How It Has Worked for Them

Marty Grunder, founder of Grunder Landscaping Company in Dayton, Ohio, credits strategic planning with the success of his twenty-seven-year-old company: "Planning has enabled me to recognize opportunities that I otherwise would not have seen. It has helped me focus my team on what the three to five most important objectives are. We call them *critical success factors* (CSFs). As a result of planning, I successfully entered the irrigation business. On the other hand, my board challenged me and kept me from entering into other businesses that did not fit our mission and vision statement.

---

### Writing a Plan

There are many valuable books and websites to teach business owners how to write strategic plans. Talk to other business owners or hire a competent business coach to help you get started. While I'm not going to spend much time on the mechanics of writing a plan, I want to share four steps of strategic

planning that have been critical for my company: analysis, mission

statements, action plans, and execution.


**Analysis**

To know what your plan should be, you must first analyze your

business, the industry, your market, and any other trends that may

influence the future of your company. I invite my board of advisors, my

leadership team, and outside consultants to McAfee strategic planning

sessions. Assemble a board of advisors who will challenge you to stretch

further than you think possible, provide fresh perspectives, and seek

answers and solutions that you and your team just can't deliver alone.

These strategic planning sessions are often daylong meetings where

we dig into the future of the company, discussing and researching our

competition, our demographics, our market opportunities, and any

perceived challenges. We always perform or update our SWOT analysis so

we can examine our strengths, weaknesses, opportunities, and threats.

SWOT analysis is a common practice in businesses, and it is an effective

one.

Speaking from personal experience, the SWOT analysis has saved

McAfee from additional costly mistakes. For example, having our own

sheet metal shop was listed as an opportunity on our SWOT analysis for

three years, but when we started to outgrow the capacity of the sheet metal

shop we were using, the fact that we didn't have our own fabrication shop

was quickly recognized as a weakness. As we planned to start up the new

division, our strong sense of urgency made things happen quickly. We

chose to start one from scratch so we could maintain our level of growth

and to sustain our culture. Had we not kept a critical eye on that part of our

business, we could have been hit with a major delay in the fabrication of

sheet metal and a loss of installations. Instead, we were able to create a

profitable new business for our company that fit snugly into our plan. Not

only were we using the shop for our own sheet metal needs, but it was also

a reliable revenue source because we utilized it to provide a great service

to other HVAC, roofing, and machine shop companies in our area.

**The Mission**

During your analysis, you also need to craft or revisit your mission and vision statements. Ask yourself this: Are your statements the right ones for today, and will they take you into tomorrow?

We review our mission and vision statements annually to make sure they still fit our plan. At McAfee, our mission statement is "Leading in air quality one home at a time." To help you understand how this reflects our dream for the business, let's break it down word for word:

**"LEADING"**: We want to dominate our residential market. We don't want to be just another mediocre business. We want to *lead*.

**"AIR QUALITY"**: This encompasses all parts of heating and air. Using this phrase broadens what we do to include heating, cooling, filtration, and air purification.

**"ONE HOME AT A TIME"**: Ninety-seven percent of our business is residential, so obviously the word "home" needs to be in our mission statement, but "one home at a time"? What does that connote? It reminds us — and our customers — that we are committed to taking care of EACH customer's needs thoroughly, promptly, and with quality, one home at a time.

A mission statement needs to be short and to the point, which also makes it easy for each team member to memorize. Our mission statement keeps us focused on work we do best. You can ask anyone in our company what our mission statement is: It's that engrained in our culture. The entire strategic plan should underpin this mission.

**Action Plan**

With the mission statement in place, now is the time to put in motion the steps to meet it. The *action plan* is how those strategic goals will be accomplished. It could include tactics, responsibilities, timelines, and budgets — the practical steps to reaching your dream.

Action plans detail what needs to happen to reach each goal. For example, what would it take to grow by 15 percent in the next year? You might need to hire three more people, buy two more trucks, and put another manager in place.

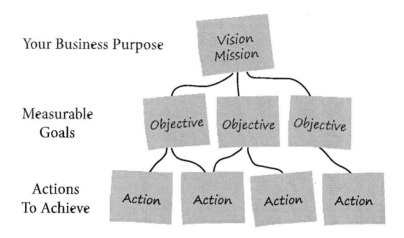

Your Business Purpose — Vision / Mission

Measurable Goals — Objective, Objective, Objective

Actions To Achieve — Action, Action, Action, Action

Your action plan sets specific steps in line to help you meet your goals. It is the key to becoming proactive instead of reactive. This part of your planning helps to shape the day-to-day work of your leadership team.

You can create a task list and action items, team goals to revisit at staff meetings, and individual goals to discuss at one-on-one meetings. It's a good idea to use the SMART goal-setting format:

**Specific**

**Measurable**

**Achievable**

**Realistic**

**Timely**

## Executing Your Plan

Writing your plan is a good start, but let's take it to the next level. It is just as important to actively follow and fine-tune a strategy after all of the major writing and planning is over. You wouldn't take the time to program your car GPS and then never listen to it or look at the screen, would you? Likewise, would you take the time to make a grocery list and then never pull it out of your pocket at the store? You might get to where you intended to go or remember most of your groceries, but you'll be frustrated, take some unnecessary turns along the way, and not have enough food for the week. Following the plan will help you avoid these issues.

Having a strong strategic plan for your dream is freeing; it takes those lofty goals and makes them achievable. That, in turn, will allow you to dream and accomplish bigger dreams than you ever thought possible.

**Questions for Reflection**

1. What is your dream?

_____

_____

_____

_____

2. Do you have a time and place to meditate on it? Where and when? If not, set one now.

_____

_____

_____

3. Are you following your plan, or is it a nice document filed away somewhere?

_____

_____

_____

_____

4. Do you have strategy sessions? Are the right people at the table?

_____

_____

_____

_____

5. Who is holding you accountable?

_____

_____

_____

_____

**Chapter Two**

**Be Teachable**

"Listen to advice and accept instruction, and in the end you will be wise."

~ Proverbs 19:20 (NIV)

In June of 2007, I made one of the best decisions in the history of my company: I assembled a board of advisors, comprised of three people whose knowledge in business compensated for areas in which I lacked know-how. They were interested in my success and willing to push me beyond my own capabilities. Our first meeting was both exciting and scary. I gladly shared my story with them so they could understand my business, and they had a lot of questions for me. Certainly, it was a draining experience, but I left challenged, knowing it would change the course of my business.

For this type of counsel to take shape, I had to be teachable. I had to be humble and open to their wisdom. There was no room for ego. I encouraged them to be tough on me, to question my thinking and challenge my decisions. Having a teachable spirit has been critical to my business success. But what does it mean to be teachable?

First, you must open yourself up to wisdom from a variety of sources: continuing education classes, your staff, your customers, books and resources, industry leaders, and business coaches. I've read hundreds of business books, but if I wasn't open to really learning from what the authors had to say, they would have done me no good whatsoever. In spite of what I have learned from all of those books, though, none have been as critical to my business as setting up a board.

Clay Mathile, former owner of the well-known Iams pet nutrition company, is noted as saying he wouldn't open a popcorn stand in Courthouse Square without setting up an advisory board first. It's just that important.

**Finding the Right Advisors**

In the 1988 movie *Tucker: The Man and His Dream*, Jeff Bridges plays the part of the great entrepreneur Preston Tucker. He is required to hire a board of directors with prestigious names to allow his company, The Tucker Corporation, to excel and go public. Robert Bennington chaired the board and ended up taking over the company. He then vetoed every great idea that Tucker came up with. This board, with the help of Congress, put Tucker right out of business. This example is NOT what I am talking about; these were NOT the right advisors, as Tucker learned the hard way.

Some of you may be thinking you already have this issue under control — that you have good people and don't need any help, and certainly not from outsiders. Or perhaps you think boards are for bigger companies. Maybe you're asking, "How in the world could I attract or afford people with any interest in my small outfit?" I thought the same way once, but if you want your business to really accelerate, you may want to reconsider. Will Rogers quipped, "Even if you are on the right track, you'll get run over if you just sit there."

Recruiting a board of advisors requires careful thought. The company should select different advisors for different areas of expertise. What are your weaknesses? Finances, marketing, team-building, human resources, strategic-planning, or operations? The outside board members should offset your weak areas. Some advisors may be recruited to provide added credibility. Well-known business leaders in your area can be especially helpful. My present board consists of three very skilled, very successful businesspeople. One is a successful owner and great national leader in the home improvement industry; another is a human resources expert who assisted in most of the hiring for the Iams Company; and the third is a former owner of a manufacturing company, with a specialty in developing the core operations. I also have some great mentors in my industry, and I rely on them when it comes to industry-specific matters. Although I value and respect them, I know the things that work for their companies won't necessarily work for mine. My board brings new and fresh ideas that fit my company.

Although your relationship may be very good with your vendors, banker, attorney, and accountant, it is not recommended that you position these people on your board. Why? Put simply, because a potential board member should have no desire to promote or generate income for their firms. Rather, they should aim to help your company perform at a higher level. Don't discount your vendors, bankers, attorneys, and accountants, though, as excellent resources to identify prospects for your board. Consider up-to-date retired executives, college business professors, or senior executives from other companies who have a proven track record of being the best.

**Frequently Asked Questions (FAQs) About Starting a
Board of Advisors**

o    **How many people should serve on my board?**
     Three on average, and no more than four.
o    **How much should I pay them?** Depending on the size of
     your company, payment for board members ranges from
     $400 to $1,000 per meeting. However, good board
     members don't serve for the purpose of making money. If
     they have an asking price up front, I recommend you don't
     use them. Your payment to them is just to show your
     appreciation.
o    **How often should we meet?** Three to four times a
     year is recommended.
o    **Should I have a contract with each member?** Yes! A
     two-year contract makes it easy for the person to leave your
     board. Be sure to include an attendance policy in the
     contract. With a small board, it's important that everyone is
     able to attend. If one of my board members can't make a
     meeting, we simply reschedule, because each member is
     that important.

- o **Where should we meet?** Find a nice, neutral space. Your CPA or attorney may allow you to use or rent their conference room A Chamber of Commerce or other industry association to which you belong may also be a good spot. If a friend has a nice office or meeting space, offer to pay them to use the space occasionally.
- o **Do you need to talk to your board members between meetings?** Avoid hounding them, but definitely call on them as resources when necessary. Many issues can be resolved by a quick e-mail exchange. We also sometimes have short, impromptu meetings if an issue comes up that I need help with.
- o **Do the board members have any rights in your company?** No! Remember, they are in place to help you with your company, not to run it or make ultimate decisions.

**What a Board Provides**

Before I had a board, I didn't realize how much I needed one. They have brought to me accountability, resources, and a challenge that has pushed our company to new heights and a more stable future.

The accountability they provide is crucial. I know the goals I set will be brought before me again. I also know there are three people who aren't going to let me get away with making unwise decisions. Without a board, I made poor decisions because I didn't have that level of accountability.

**How it Has Worked for Them**

Mark Grunkenmeyer, CEO of Buckeye Ecocare in Centerville, Ohio, explains how his board is helping the company to tackle one of the biggest challenges in its history. "Our board of advisors is guiding our family through a successful transition from our first generation to the second. Family personalities and generational differences, together with the struggles that most small businesses face, can create challenges beyond what most companies face. The board has directed all stockholders to exercise patience and carefully review all stock transfer options, along with many other recommendations to ensure a smooth transition of ownership. Without a board, we would be a ship without a sail–still floating, but not moving on course!"

My board challenges me to do better. They help me see things in ways I never would have previously considered. They give me homework and help me set realistic, achievable, important goals for my company and myself.

For instance, before I had a board, I didn't know much about metrics. I knew hard work pays off and that we were growing, but whenever anyone asked me why, I had no specific answer. My board and I have discovered together the key performance indicators we should measure, such as our net profit, our performance index, and the residential-to-commercial ratio of our business. As we started to understand where our growth came from, we were able to target our marketing and be more proactive to keep growing. At my board's urging for more metrics, I added a business analyst to our staff. Every day, she provides the metrics I need to make decisions. Without a board pressing me for those details, I might have never taken that vital step.

My board also prompted a dramatic change in our hiring procedures. I went to them when we were having trouble hiring a service technician. The human resources expert on my board called us out on a weakness. That discussion opened the door for an overhaul of our recruiting, interviewing, and decision-making process. At the time, we performed one or two relatively loose interviews before making a decision. Now, we have a list of specific questions conducted by various staff members for the applicant. If need be, I'm the last one to interview an applicant.

Without having an HR expert on the board to help improve our processes, we wouldn't have hired some of the talented people we have on staff today—people who fit our culture and are more likely to stay.

By being teachable, you can push your company beyond your own limits. Everyone has blind spots. What matters is that you recognize them and pay attention to those who can see more clearly where you are steering.

## Other Ways To Be Teachable

As valuable as a board can be, there are specific situations where entrepreneurs will need a different style of help. If you think of your board as a head coach, you can consider a business coach more like a position coach who targets a specific part of your business. If you are setting out to hit a particularly challenging goal, it can be a great motivator to hire a business coach who has accomplished that specific task. The ideal candidate is someone from your industry who has been more successful than you, someone who has grappled with the same challenges. A business coach doesn't always require a face-to-face meeting; you can often talk on the phone or via e-mail. Touching base at least once a week to review your progress is recommended.

I once had a coach who made me put deadlines on several goals. To challenge me, he had me write him a check for $10,000. He promised to send the check back to me if I met my goal by the deadline; however, if I didn't meet my goal, he would mail the check to someone who I would least want to have it! Knowing that $10,000 of my money hung in the balance pushed me to listen to his advice and work toward those goals. Thankfully, I hit the goal and rescued my money from falling into undesirable hands. I challenge you to try a similar approach — and it only works if you choose a dollar amount big enough to hurt.

You can get away with building your business on your own, for a while. Truly lifting your business beyond your own capabilities, however, requires opening up to the wisdom of others. When you are teachable and willing to implement what you learn, you will watch your dream come closer to reality each day.

## Questions for Reflection

1. Are you teachable? How do you know?

_____

_____

_____

_____

2. What keeps you from opening up and listening to instruction?

_____

_____

_____

_____

3. Do you have a board of advisors?

_____

_____

_____

_____

4. If not, who might serve on your board?

_____

_____

_____

_____

5. If you have a board, are you getting the most out of the experience? Are they providing the accountability, challenges and resources that you need?

_____

_____

_____

_____

6. Identify three things a business coach could help you improve in the next year.

_____

_____

_____

_____

**Chapter Three**

**Be a Coach**

"Leadership is a matter of having people look at you and gain confidence,
seeing how you react. If you're in control, they're in control."

~ Tom Landry

When I worked at Firestone, I had a boss who could be described

as a classic micromanager. He enjoyed standing over us, watching as we

worked, the problem with that being that he was really just in the way.

When he backed off, we worked much faster. From that experience, I

learned that the best managers give you space to succeed — and fail — on

your own. They are coaches, not bosses. Instead of micromanaging, they

step back and see the entire field. They empower their team to lead and

work in their own ways, while still carrying out the team's values and

mission. This equates to much better results.

In my own experience, I have also learned that every leader has a

tendency to micromanage. When the buck stops with you and your name is

on the door or the billboard, it's hard to give up control. Over time, I have

evolved from a boss into a coach. Being a coach means treating your staff like a team rather than employees. To do that, you must learn to appreciate those you work with and not just see them as bodies or numbers on a payroll. You have to really know them as people and individuals so you can develop an understanding of what truly motivates them (which, in most cases, goes beyond a paycheck). You have to trust your people to do jobs you used to do, even if they do them differently than you did. You have to be flexible and humble enough to give them that freedom. If you do all of this, you will be a coach, and that is really what your team needs.

**How To Be a Coach**

What kind of leader are you? Or better yet, what kind of leader do you want to be? There are myriad leadership styles, and many a book has been written on the subject to help business leaders identify their own styles and adapt the characteristics of successful leaders. For me, the Hersey-Blanchard Situational Leadership model has best helped me shape and define my path toward being a coach in this business. The Hersey-Blanchard model carves out four leadership styles, dubbed S1 to S4. Each is suited for a different type of situation, although in my opinion and experience, leaders must be able to operate at an S3-S4 level in order for their business to thrive and grow. Let's take a look at how the Hersey-Blanchard model defines these styles:

**S1: Telling** — Characterized by one-way communication. The leader says, "Do," and everyone does.

**S2: Selling** — While the leader is still providing the direction, s/he now uses two-way communication, while controlling the process by influencing (selling) the individual or group to take the leader's point of view.

**S3: Participating** — This encompasses shared decision-making. The task is accomplished more by the individual and their ideas rather than the leaders.

**S4: Delegating** — The leader is still involved in decisions; however, the process and responsibility is passed to the individual or group. The leader stays involved only to monitor progress.

Let's walk through an example of how each leader would handle the same situation in their business. Those in the HVAC industry will quickly recognize the following scenario:

The Environmental Protection Agency (EPA) orders a phase-out of the R-22 refrigerant and the introduction of the non-ozone depleting refrigerant R410-A. HVAC companies are faced with the decision of how to implement this regulation in their businesses. It is a costly changeover, and even though it is to be done in phases and not all at once, it will eventually become the new way of doing business.

Now let's see how those different leadership styles play out in real life and how each leadership style responds.

**S1 Leader:** S1 leaders make the decision without any input. Likely, they say, "I'm not changing until I have to." They simply wait until the units using R-22 refrigerant are no longer available and then make the change. Or, like I did at the time, they just decide to upgrade to the new. Regardless, they never discuss the topic with their staff.

**S2 Leader:** Typical S2 leaders are quick to make up their minds but still ask for ideas. They explain the cost and training issues and persuade everyone to ride it out. They go through the exercise of asking for input but still persuade their staff to go along with their idea anyway.

**S3 Leader:** An S3 leader brings all the pros and cons to the table, breaks into groups, and lets the team decide. The leader gives it his or her blessing but isn't involved in the hashing out of the decision.

**S4 Leader:** The leadership team has a meeting, but the S4 leader doesn't attend. Instead, they remain uninvolved and are briefed on the decision after the matter has been settled.

Every level of growth requires a different level of leadership. I alternate between S3 and S4. However, S2 is also a comfortable place for me; it's easy for me to persuade, which gives me that comfort of trying to convince others to accept my opinion. However, for the sake of growing our company, I have pushed to be more of an S4. Successful companies have S3 or S4 leaders. Please note, though, that you need to be flexible in whatever leadership style you choose. There are times when you need to go back to an S1, directly instructing employees how to handle a situation. It all depends on the maturity of the employee and the particular situation (Hersey and Blanchard offer a corresponding model based on the maturity level of employees, from M1 to M4).

An S1 can be very successful with six or fewer employees. They can still work in the business, be hands on, and call all the shots, and many are happy doing that. The problem with an S1 leader is that s/he rarely takes the time to work on the business. I was an S1 for much of my company's startup years. I was elbow deep in scheduling, marketing, running service, selling, and trying to manage appointments. Slowly, by hiring talented people to do those jobs, I was able to focus on the strategic view of our business. When you are doing everything in your company, you don't have the time or energy to dream about where your company will be tomorrow. Many S1 leaders do not have a business that operates smoothly. Instead, they have what I call an out-of-control baby, and I know firsthand that it's a full-time job baby-sitting all day.

Because my dream was to grow, I knew lingering in the S1 leadership style wasn't an option. Even early on, I knew I didn't want to stay in the garage. One of my first trainees, Chris B., left us to go to a heating and air training school out of the state. When he returned a year later, he asked about being promoted to the position of service technician. I was hesitant at first, but he persuaded me to put him out in the field on his own so he could have a chance to prove himself. I was still being an S1, stifling my growth and his because I did not want to release him on his own.

After much persuasion, though, I promoted Chris, and it wasn't long before he became our go-to guy for troubleshooting. I got better at letting go as time went on. It really boils down to trust; I've learned to trust my people to do a good job. Most people want to excel, and we only have to give them a chance to do so. Communication between Chris and me became two-way; I bounced ideas off of him and vice versa. I'm glad to say that Chris is still here at McAfee today, serving as our very capable lead service technician, and he has trained many along the way.

Little did I realize, though, that I was in the process of moving away from an S1 style and becoming an S2. About six years into the business, I was still rotating on call to run emergency service appointments, a twenty-four/seven chore. Finally, after much frustration and stress, I gathered my two technicians and told them I could no longer be on call. I shared with them that it was too difficult to run the business effectively while staying out all night working.

Each time I took steps to empower my workers and free myself from the daily tasks of our business, I experienced more freedom to focus on the strategic plan. It freed me up to attend classes and conferences, which proved to be valuable learning opportunities. Today, I can take what I learn and share with other HVAC leaders. Do you feel you're too busy to attend conferences and/or seminars? S1 leaders are too consumed with putting out little fires to take the time to focus on the big picture. They can't take time for their families or their own physical or mental health. One of the byproducts I experienced of the change in leadership was that it allowed me to spend more time with my family. S1 leaders find it difficult to take a vacation because they never think they have time for one. All work and no play really does make Johnny a dull boy, and it will eventually burn you out.

As a Christian, I often look to my Bible for guidance. It's one of the few things I take with me to my "dreaming sessions." My Leadership Bible deals with most, if not all, business issues we come across.

On the topic of coaching, we can learn a lot from Moses and his father-in-law Jethro. In Exodus 18, Jethro visits Moses and observes him settling disputes among the people of Israel all day and night. It eats up Moses's time and energy, and Jethro suggests an alternate plan:

> The next day, Moses took his seat to serve as judge
> for the people, and they stood around him from morning
> till evening.[13] When his father-in-law saw all that

Moses was doing for the people, he said, "What is this you

are doing for the people? Why do you alone sit as judge,

while all these people stand around you from morning till

evening?"[14]

Moses answered him, "Because the people come

to me to seek God's will.[15] Whenever they have a dispute,

it is brought to me, and I decide between the parties and

inform them of God's decrees and instructions."[16]

Moses's father-in-law replied, "What you are

doing is not good.[17] You and these people who come to

you will only wear yourselves out. The work is too heavy

for you; you cannot handle it alone.[18] Listen now to me,

and I will give you some advice, and may God be with

you.[19] You must be the people's representative before God

and bring their disputes to Him. Teach them His decrees

and instructions and show them the way they are to live

and how they are to behave.[20] But select capable men from

all the people — men who fear God, trustworthy men who

hate dishonest gain — and appoint them as officials over

thousands, hundreds, fifties, and tens.[21] Have them serve

as judges for the people at all times but have them bring every difficult case to you; the simple cases they can decide themselves. That will make your load lighter, because they will share it with you.[22] If you do this and God so commands, you will be able to stand the strain, and all these people will go home satisfied."[23]

Moses listened to his father-in-law and did everything he said.[24] He chose capable men from all Israel and made them leaders of the people, officials over thousands, hundreds, fifties, and tens.[25] They served as judges for the people at all times. The difficult cases they brought to Moses, but the simple ones they decided themselves.[26]

What a great lesson in leadership! Listen to the wisdom in Verses 22 and 23: "That will make your load lighter, because they will share it with you. If you do this and God so commands, you will be able to stand the strain, and all these people will go home satisfied." Isn't that what running a business should be all about? Satisfying customers and employees and "standing the strain" of the heavy load of being a business

owner? Definitely!

## Empowering Your Team

Like Moses, you must empower others to lead. If you don't give

your leadership team the freedom to lead, you will stifle growth with low

morale, slow decision-making, and fear. At McAfee, five team leaders

report to me, and the rest of our team reports to them or another manager.

I hire people who manage differently than me. They know the

values and mission of our company, and they've been trained in our way

of doing business, though how they carry out the means to get there might

be different than my approach. I call this the "same cake, different icing."

There is no need for me to watch over them all day, nor do I have to have

constant contact. Every Monday, they send me a report, a snapshot of the

highs and lows of the previous week and opportunities for the coming

days. In the past, I held the reins much tighter. As I gave responsibilities to

employees, I would tell them to call me in the morning and in the evening,

meaning I spent hours on the phone for updates. Now, I only ask them to

call in an emergency they can't manage. They also know they can call each other first to work out problems before bringing it to me, and that empowerment and trust builds a stronger team.

---

### How it Has Worked for Them

As president of the eighty-five-year-old industrial gas equipment company, RexArc International Inc., Jim Bowman has learned the importance of training. "Think through and formulate a clear career path for the person you are looking to hire. Understand that they will only be 70 percent to 80 percent qualified for the position when you hire them but have a plan to develop them to the 100 percent level and then be sure you know where their next step will be in their career. Evaluate their capacity to help get there prior to hiring them. There are also professional testing agencies that will help you measure their capacity for growth."

---

### Building a Culture by Training Your Team

What keeps many leaders stuck at an S1 level? Most often, it's fear of letting others take control in the business. As the leader of a company — especially if you are the founder — you know that no one will ever take your business as personally as you do. Of course there is risk involved

when you let others make decisions and represent your company, but it's a

risk that must be taken. The key is to train your people properly so that you

can build a common business culture within your team.

First, you must recognize what your culture is. A company's

*culture* is a blend of values and beliefs developed over time. It's the way

we do business, and it's an integral part of building a brand, which we'll

talk about in the next chapter. At McAfee, building a culture and training

go hand in hand. We begin explaining our culture, the "McAfee Way," as

early as the very first job interview. I didn't realize until several years into

running the company that I had established a very particular way of

operating. Once I realized it, we began to intentionally build it into

training. In fact, we launched McAfee University (McU), complete with

our own t-shirts, as a way to formally train our employees on the principles

of our culture.

Just as coaches train their sports teams through practice, so must

business leaders. You can't move to the higher levels of leadership until

you have coached your employees through mock situations and explained

your expectations to them. Much of our internal training happens through

role-playing. Our service technicians go through these mock exercises to reinforce the people skills we want our team to carry into client homes. We set up various scenarios: greeting a man, greeting a woman, where to park, when to put on your shoe protectors, how to deal with dogs, and how to set the right tone in the first two minutes of the appointment. Our sales team members — "Comfort Advisors" at McAfee — practice learning to sell to various generations and demographics, whether it be a single man or woman, the elderly, or a young family. Our veteran staff members play the roles and pepper the trainee with all the questions we get on the job from day to day. Our method of sales reinforces our own particular set of values and expectations.

Our customer service representatives are also thoroughly trained on telephone skills, from their tone of voice to how to politely take control of the call. We believe so strongly in professional phone skills that we require two weeks of training before they are even allowed to answer a phone and put a customer on hold. We believe in a live person answering the phone, so we make sure each employee is trained in our specific method of greeting customers. Intentional coaching helps our employees be more successful in their jobs because they know the parameters they are expected to work within. You don't have to copy our culture to be successful, but you do need to find your own way and stick to it.

We invest in training throughout all seasons because we want to continuously improve. Some owners fear that if they train, employees will leave and take their new skills to a competitor, but we fear the opposite: What if we don't train them properly and thoroughly and they stay onboard with us?

Another realm of training is to help all of our employees understand the bigger picture of our business.

Our team plays a competitive board game called TOBGOB: The Open Book Game of Business (www.tobgob.com). I designed this game with the intention of helping team members think like owners. We break into teams to compete, and each team experiences the reality of running a business. This is a fun and challenging way to foster a competitive spirit and help everyone better appreciate the many decisions required to effectively run a business.

Over time, the continual training of your staff on the principles of your culture will transform your business and your leadership style. Start today by identifying the hallmarks of your culture so you can instill them in your people. Make a training plan. You will all be better for it in the end.

**Knowing Your Staff**

We have already touched on this lightly, but it bears repeating: If you are going to be an effective, competent coach, you have to know your team. This starts during the interview process. We ask applicants questions designed to reveal what is important to them, such as the books they've read recently or the amount of vacation they received at their last job. We give them a stack of cards with an important value of our company on each card — such as integrity, honesty, and family — and we ask interviewees to arrange the cards in the order of most importance to them; then they narrow it down to five and ultimately down to the two most important. Why? Because it is important for us to know what motivates the people who work at McAfee. We even take a peek at their car: Since past behavior is a known indicator of future behavior in most cases, if they keep their own vehicle clean inside and out, we can safely assume they'll probably be able to keep our trucks and equipment clean and well maintained.

Last year, we had our employees fill out a survey listing what they needed from their company. Job security topped that list, and this taught us more about how to work with our team. That simple survey prevented us from trying to coach them blindly.

## Knowing Your Style

As important as it is to know your team, it's also crucial to know yourself. Have you ever thought of asking your staff or leadership team to describe your leadership style and how it impacts the business? Do they see you the way you see yourself? When I took the time to ask my leadership team to tell me how they perceive my leadership style, this was some of their feedback:

## Director of Field Operations (Thirteen Years with McAfee)

**How does Greg's leadership style play out for you in working with him?** Greg is like a coach. He is the head coach who relies on his assistant coaches to take care of the day-to-day duties. Greg empowers us to make decisions whether they're right, wrong, or indifferent. As part of the leadership team, we send Greg weekly reports every Monday, no later than nine a.m., to keep him briefed on what is going on. He enjoys making suggestions, or he might recommend doing something differently. Since I've been here, his leadership style has changed for the better. When the team was smaller, Greg used to be a micromanager, but today he's not like that. He empowers us to make decisions and to live with those decisions, whatever they may be.

**How does that help you in coaching your own team?** After

working with Greg all these years, I've tried to mirror many of his

leadership skills. Although there is a lot to learn, I'm a work in progress.

Allowing my team to make many of their own decisions keeps them

thinking and on their toes. Empowering them allows them to make their

own decisions and learn from them.

**How has McAfee differed from other places you have worked?**

I worked for a smaller HVAC company right out of high school. It lacked

leadership and structure and is now out of business. Let's just say it's a

night-and-day difference. Even though McAfee was a young/small

company when I started here, we had structure. It's much easier to work

for a company when you know what's expected of you. Over the years,

Greg and team members have developed a culture that is very professional

and lasting. I would not want it any other way.


**Office Manager (Ten Years with McAfee)**

When I came to McAfee, there were eight employees, nine

including Greg. I was the first person hired as a manager. Not long after

being hired, I asked him, "How would you feel about me signing the checks and you looking at a check register report for approval?" For a person who owns his own business, it's a leap of faith to let go of your baby and trust that someone is getting your money where it needs to go. As an owner, you have to let your people be able to do things and trust that they can and will handle those things the way you would want. He no longer does the things he used to do. Now, he lets go and lets his leaders do them!

**Does this make things easier for you here?** Sure! If we had to go to Greg for every decision, we would not have grown. For me, it's the ability to say to my staff, "I want you to handle this project," or "Okay, yes, you can be off work tomorrow." I do not have to check with Greg about everything first. I may bounce things off of Greg or other leadership team members, but the decisions are mine, and he lets us run our departments. When things go wrong, that's when we are able to go to Greg and say things like, "What do you think?" or, "How could I have done this differently?" He sometimes lets us go ahead and make mistakes. After all, that's how we learn.

**What is the communication like between Greg and his leaders?** You can always go to him and say, "Hey, I'm having this problem. Here's what I think I should do. Am I on the right page, or is there a better way?" I can learn from Greg's experience, or we can discuss it and come up with a better solution. Accounting wise, he trusts me to be able to do my job, because he's not an accountant. You hire good people to do those jobs so you don't have to watch over them every minute.

**How is it different from other places you have worked?** I have been in the working world for forty years, yet I have never worked with a company that has a stronger pattern and plan for growth. We have specific goals — from eight people to where we are today is big for us. We have many more systems in place and continue to improve daily. My direct benefit in accounting is that we pay all of our bills on time, all the time and the integrity that comes with it. Vendors are happy to have us as a customer because we always pay promptly. Employees know they are going to be paid. It's nice to be a part of that kind of upstanding culture. When it all rolls down, at the end of the day, the McAfee name is on the door. It's entrusting your people to make decisions on your behalf. It's like taking care of your child. It's an evolution for him as well.

**Service Coordinator (Eight Years with McAfee)**

The Leadership Team is empowered to make decisions. Right or

wrong, we make them nonetheless. We just learn from our mistakes and

move on. Decision-making helps us grow individually as leaders. It helps

us build on the tools needed to take care of the day-to-day operations. This

has allowed Greg to work more *on* the company and not so much *in* the

company. We are given the opportunity to grow as leaders, to work on our

decision-making, to work with our team, and to improve our

communication with other leaders. Greg makes it a point to seek out our

opinions regularly and involve us in strategic business planning. This

creates a team environment, one in which we know we are valued. There

are no lone rangers here; everything we do is a team process.

Understanding Greg's actions and his thinking has greatly

influenced my growth since day one. In retrospect, I can now see the

different leadership styles he took with me as time ran its course. When I

first started, Greg took more of a direct, telling style of coaching with me.

It was, "This is what you do... This is how you do it... Don't do it that

way... That is the wrong way to do it." I was micromanaged, and I

admittedly probably needed that at the time. As I evolved in my position

and in my understanding of the company, Greg's leadership style evolved right along with me. He became less directive and let me figure more

things out on my own. I began to make my own decisions, along with my

own mistakes. Personally, as a leader, I feel you must be able to recognize

what style of leadership you need to take based on the individual and

based on the task. Greg does this very well. Today, I find myself

mimicking this same approach.

For instance, when I'm training a new Customer Service

Representative (CSR), I am more direct and oversee all tasks to ensure

they are being carried out properly. I am more apt to encourage our

seasoned CSRs to figure more things out on their own.

**How is working at McAfee different than other places?** The

culture is everything here. We know who we are, what we do, and where

we're going. We choose not to do things the way many other companies

do. We're unique. When anyone new comes in, it takes a while to learn

and embrace the McAfee Way of doing business. We are very structured

and organized, and expectations are high. We take it for granted that

people are going to be on time and ready to work when they get here. I

know there are other companies out there having trouble just getting their

employees to show up in the morning. Here, we don't have those kinds of problems because it's just expected. Everyone on this staff knows that

that's the McAfee Way.

A few years back, I left McAfee for about a year to work for

another company. My new employer did not share the same sense of

urgency, the culture, or the guiding principles I had grown accustomed to.

There was no direction, no course. Honestly, before I left McAfee, I

wondered, *Are those things really that important?* I can tell you now that

the answer is a resounding "YES!" They are that important, and everything

matters! In my absence, I developed a whole new appreciation for McAfee

and its operations. I realized that those were not just McAfee principles

anymore; they had become my own. Once this realization was made, I

knew I simply could not work for any other company.


**Comfort Advisor/Sales Representative (One and a Half Years with**

**McAfee)**

**How is McAfee different than other places you have worked?**

It is very different. I have worked for family-owned companies, as well as

large corporations. I like the structure and organization of the corporate

environment. I also like the close personal relationships and fun you can have working for a family-run business. You get the best of both worlds here, even if it's not the easiest place to work because a lot is expected.

We are a very structured, streamlined business, but we are also a very close team. I think what makes us so different is that we operate at such high levels but have a lot of fun doing what we do here on a day-to-day basis.

**How does Greg's leadership style play out in your relationship with him?** Greg coaches from experience. We get extensive training here. It is easy to learn from him because you know he has been there before, and you can really feel the passion he has for what we do. He is a very good salesman and has taught me how sales are done here. I have learned a lot, but I have also run into some obstacles. The obstacles have taught me more than anything. Greg has used these obstacles as learning experiences and opportunities for me to grow. He is always willing to listen to my feedback and ideas, and he always encourages open communication. Through this, not only have I become a better salesman, but a better person as well.

**How does that help you carry out your job?** I'm more efficient now. I'm better at what I do because I have learned through experience.

Once you get used to the culture here, you just adopt it and run with it.
That's what makes us so good!


**Business Analyst (Three Years with McAfee)**

**How is McAfee different from other work places?** The
leadership team is the biggest difference from other places I have been
employed. Our leadership team provides representation for each
department in the company. We meet regularly and discuss each
department. We are able to bounce ideas off each other. The input we
receive from the team helps us make better, more informed decisions. We
form plans together and implement them.

My position is another major difference at McAfee. At the places
where I worked in the past, performance was measured with opinions,
based only on things that recently happened. At McAfee, we use *actual*
measurements to support employee evaluations and to make important
decisions. We do not leave things up to chance. I research our company
history, sales trends, and weather patterns. Greg is willing to take risks, but
at the same time, he spends time to research what works. He often calls a
leadership meeting to run a new idea by everyone. He listens to five other

perspectives before he makes a final decision. As leaders, this makes us feel important, and we get to share in the successes.

At McAfee, the financial results are shared with the company. At each company meeting, Greg allows me twenty minutes to present this information to the team. I go over the prior month's results. We discuss our successes and our failures. We also discuss our goals and our plan to achieve those goals. Everyone has a chance to be part of the plan. McAfee is the first company I have worked for that openly shares the financial standing with the entire company.

**Questions for Reflection**

1. Where are you operating on the Hersey-Blanchard Situational Leadership model? What will it take to get to the next level?

_____

_____

_____

_____

2. What are the characteristics of your company culture? Are you training your employees on these principles?

_____

_____

_____

_____

3. How do your team members describe your leadership style? If you can't answer this question, ask! If you don't ask, you'll never know!

_____

_____

_____

_____

4. Ask your team leaders to describe your company culture.

_____

_____

_____

_____

*The entire McAfee Fleet in 1991; combined value was $3,600. Neither truck had air conditioning.*

*"The Garage," a 24x24 building, half-office, half-warehouse, and no plumbing! We operated from there nearly five years, generating nearly a million dollars in revenue the final year.*

*The McAfee Headquarters consists of 11,000 sq. ft. of offices, training rooms, classrooms and a Dream Room. It was built yesterday for tomorrow and is able to handle growth for many years to come.*

*The 8:00-8:00 concept was conceived in an effort to conveniently serve customers at times when they are home. To date, this branding and marketing strategy has proven to be the best in McAfee history.*

*What separates a good company from a great company can be the amount of training they invest in. We spend thousands of dollars in training each year, both internally and externally.*

*Our regular monthly Saturday morning meetings are designed to be fun, upbeat, educational, and team oriented. We've increased the size of our training room three times in the past five years. Much innovation has come from these meetings.*

*The McAfee Board of Advisors: Anita W., Steve L., and Michael K., participating in a meeting at Aileron and assisting me in next year's strategy. I am blessed to have such a great team of advisors.*

*Here is an example of branding myself with my logo and truck. The quality we portray is quickly recognized by  past, present, and future consumers.*

## Chapter Four

## Be Known

"Today you are you, that is truer than true.
There is no one alive who is you-er than you."

~ Dr. Seuss

When I started McAfee, no one knew me. I didn't have family in Dayton; I hadn't even lived here long. I had to create a name for myself in the industry. It was part of my dream to operate a well-known company, and I wasn't satisfied operating under the radar. If I was going to take the risk of starting my own business, I was willing to do what I could to make sure everyone knew we were their best choice for residential heating and air. I don't think it was a desire rooted in ego, but rather in a competitive streak that drives me to want to win at anything I set out to do. That drive has served me well in the world of marketing.

If someone is going to use your service, they've got to know your name. It's that simple. Figuring out how to best reach current and future customers can be complicated. Who makes up your market? How do you get your message to them? Have you considered television, radio, newspapers, magazines, direct mail, online? Will you do any sponsorship? How much should you spend? Do you need an agency?

The options for advertisement and getting your name out there are endless and can be overwhelming at first. However, when you hit on the right strategy to reach existing and potential clients, it's likely your company will grow.

Marketing is a risk — at times, an expensive one. You must know right from the start that your efforts might not work. At McAfee, because of the nature of the service we provide, we are very weather driven. If I spend $50,000 on advertising, I have to understand that a significant change in the moody Ohio weather might mean I will never see that $50,000 again. A major mistake a small business makes is considering advertising an expense they cannot afford. It can take decades to build a strong word-of-mouth business. In fact, it took us ten to fifteen years to build a consistent stream of business from word-of-mouth referrals. It's a wonderful compliment to have a customer call because they've heard great things about you from a trusted friend. However, relying on word-of-mouth alone will render your business growth an even slower and arduous process. With so many options available to reach your customers directly, there's no need to leave it to chance. As trite as it is, the old adage is true: You have to spend money to make money. Annually, we budget 10 percent of our gross revenue for advertising and marketing. As we've grown, our advertising budget has increased, but not the percentage. I encourage you to set a percent of your budget for marketing annually and stick with it.

**How to Kill Your Business in Ten Easy Steps**

**1. Don't advertise.** Just pretend everyone already knows what you have to offer.

**2. Don't advertise.** Tell yourself you don't have time to spend thinking about your business.

**3. Don't advertise.** Just assume everyone already knows what you sell.

**4. Don't advertise.** Convince yourself that you've been in business so long that customers will automatically come to you.

**5. Don't advertise.** Forget that there are new potential customers who might do business with you if they were invited to do so.

**6. Don't advertise.** Forget that you have competition who is trying to attract your customers away from you.

**7. Don't advertise.** Tell yourself it costs too much and that you don't get enough out of it.

**8. Don't advertise.** Overlook the fact that advertising is an investment in selling and not an expense.

**9. Don't advertise.** Be sure not to provide an adequate advertising budget for your business.

**10. Don't advertise.** Forget that you have to keep reminding your established customers that you appreciate their business.


What's the bottom line? If you want to avoid killing your business, you have to ADVERTISE!

We started small: advertising in a local direct mail magazine and

the phone book, sponsoring a Little League team, and plastering my truck

with the company name. Now we are on television, radio, the Internet, and

other media. Over the years, we have invested in building a brand and a

successful advertising strategy. We didn't start out building a brand

intentionally; in fact, I didn't have any training in marketing when I started

my business. Most of what I have learned has been through reading books

and experience. If I can build a strong brand from scratch, so can you.


**Marketing, Advertising, and Branding**

These terms — **marketing, advertising,** and **branding** — are

often used interchangeably, but they are actually three distinct, yet

overlapping concepts. To make the most of your money, it's worth

studying the differences.

**Marketing.** This is a broad term. Just look at the American

Marketing Association's definition: "the activity, set of institutions,

and processes for creating, communicating, delivering, and exchanging

offerings that have value for customers, clients, partners, and society at

large." But what does that mean to an entrepreneur? Imagine

marketing as the overall strategy for reaching your customers. A marketing plan includes all the aspects of promotion, such as advertising,

public relations, brand identity, sales strategy, direct mail, customer

service, and community involvement. These all work in unison to

"market" your services or products and build the type of reputation you

want to be known for.

**Advertising.** One of the most important pieces of your marketing

puzzle is advertising. Paid for and controlled by the company,

advertisements focus on building brand awareness and driving sales. Ads

can be delivered through newspapers, magazines or mailings, radio,

television, or online. Knowing the demographics of your target customer is

critical to figuring out the best medium to place an advertisement.

Advertisements must work independently, while also being integrated with

the other components of your marketing plan. Too many HVAC companies

mistakenly think running a commercial on TV or the radio is all it takes,

yet they are disappointed when a rush of business doesn't follow.

Advertising can be a powerful tool, but it doesn't work in a vacuum.

**Branding.** This is very important, for it is your company's

promise to the customer. Entrepreneur.com defines it well: "It tells them

what they can expect from your products and services, and it differentiates

your offering from that of your competitors. Your brand is derived from

who you are, who you want to be, and who people perceive you to be."
You can have marketing without branding, but you can't have branding
without marketing. A branding strategy lays out who you are or who you
want to be. It should mirror the brand your customers see, feel, and touch.
Your brand strength should be measured in years and decades, not days
and months. Consistency is vital to the success of your brand. You need
the same look and same message inside and outside your company. One
part of that look is your logo — often the most visual connection anyone
has with a product or company before, after, and during a business
relationship. It should be consistent in style and color and give a
professional image.

Would it help to hire a marketing firm? Maybe. You may also
consider hiring a consultant, like myself, who has a history in the business
and can help you strategize your marketing before you ever need an
agency. Unfortunately, small businesses far too often hire huge advertising
firms they can't really afford. You don't have to look for the biggest fish
in the pond. Some smaller firms, combined with the right experience, can
be an asset to your company's marketing strategy. If you are in the service
industry, make sure the advertising firm you choose has previous
experience with service companies, as marketing can be different for
products and services.

**What's Effective?**

If your business is new or you just haven't thought about these concepts before, it can be a lot to take in. Long gone are the days of just placing an ad in the local newspaper or on the radio and waiting for your phones to start ringing. The leading businesses are savvy marketers who take advantage of many tools to reach their customers. What works best? Where should you invest? You need to know the answers to these questions.

The more you study your demographics and understand where your growth comes from, the better you'll know where and how to market and advertise. I've had to try marketing techniques or venues anywhere from six months to a year to know what works. If you can't track any return on your investment after that, it's probably not working. Pull a focus group of six to ten customers and find out what they like and didn't like about your ad. Ask yourself some questions: *Am I targeting the right audience? Is it airing enough to resonate with potential customers?*

For us, the right combination of advertising has been television, radio, and Internet. I appear in our commercials as the face of the company, and I back up our work with a personal promise: "You can count on my company because you can count on me." It's not uncommon for local business owners to appear in their own commercials, and some national brands also use their leaders on air (Papa John's founder John Schnatter, George Foreman with his grill, the late Dave Thomas of Wendy's restaurants, and late popcorn king Orville Redenbacher, just to name a few). I didn't realize how well our strategy was working, so I chose to go with another advertising firm. They created an advertising campaign that took me out of the commercials. During the year those ran, our revenue declined. Through this trial and error, we realized that changing our marketing identity so quickly was not a wise choice. We then decided to go back to the original company and get back on course. Change can work when there is a good reason and you are not modifying things just for the sake of change. I don't believe every business owner should be in his or her own commercials. If you are uncomfortable on camera or the message being sent does not produce results, it is recommended that you search for alternative talent.

Be consistent in your marketing and advertising. Your company colors, logo, and slogan should be the same across every platform so they will be recognizable over time. We all know what the Coca-Cola font looks like or what that swoop means on a pair of athletic shoes, right? Branding is your chance to differentiate your company from the rest — to set the image you want to impart.

It's important that you realize that it can take years, even decades, to build a brand, but it can take only a short time to lose it. I'm reminded of the Black and Decker story. Black and Decker built a brand known for high-quality tools used by professionals. In spite of this, the brand — and tool sales — declined when the company began branding household appliances. In 1992, the company revived their power tool sales by launching them under a new brand name — DeWALT — and built it up as a rugged, high-quality line for professional tradesman. Chances are, that old Black and Decker DustBuster from 1979 might be collecting dust somewhere in your garage or closet, but DeWALT drills are being used every day.

We want to be known as a trustworthy, professional, quality company — from the way our technicians and staff dress and speak with clients, to the networking groups we frequent, to the community service projects we support.

**Stay Ready, Stay Current**

The longer you are in business, the more you will come to find that while your marketing message may stay the same, the methods of appealing to and reaching your customers must change. Wise businesses stay current, whether it's understanding the latest technologies or figuring out what drives various generations of consumers.

For us, that has meant following our customer base online through investing in search optimization, placing paid advertisements, and developing our own mobile phone applications.

It also means quickly responding to opportunities. In 2009, the government launched an economic stimulus package that included tax incentives for those who bought high-efficiency appliances. We were the first in our market to match the government's rebate. We marketed the offer heavily and believe it allowed us to post record revenue growth even in a down economy.

One of our biggest marketing breakthroughs was a response to a change in culture. As a residential company, we have to schedule appointments when a homeowner is home, but in today's dual-income economy, that isn't always easy. In 2005, we launched an after-hours service promise. Under the marketing promotion "8:00 to 8:00 at the Same

Great Rate!'" we promised to be available from eight a.m. to eight p.m. This set us apart from the competition, and because we backed up our promise with logistical planning, we were successful in working the new hours. Today, our fastest-growing time of scheduling service is between five and eight p.m. We've added more technicians to accommodate our customers. It continues to be one of our strongest marketing points.


**Backing It Up with Brand Identity**

You can spend a million dollars on advertising and still have a failing business if your company does not live up to its promises. Your standards for customer service and work quality must match the image you portray. If we hadn't staffed our company adequately to pull off a new work schedule, we would have failed as soon as the calls started coming in. If our customer service representatives and service technicians weren't well trained in our brand identity, their actions would counteract the professional image of trust we sent to market through our ads.

---

**How It Has Worked for Them**

Louis Hobaica, president of Hobaica Services Inc., in Phoenix, Arizona, doesn't see advertising as expensive, but as a necessity. "Advertising is essential for a thriving and successful business. Whether you spend your marketing budget with your employees or with outside sources, it is essential. Marketing is like watering a plant: Water it properly, and it will thrive. Provide little or no water, and it will wither away and die! Downtimes are when you need to increase your marketing efforts, as most of your competition will slack off and you will have much better results and exposure. For any maintenance/repair/retrofit company, I recommend budgeting at least 5 percent of total sales for marketing."

---

Several companies have built gold-standard brands with their customer service and consistency. The $3.2 billion fast food restaurant chain Chick-fil-A has built its brand on its values, setting it apart from its competitors and leading to consistent, fast growth.

Founder Truett Cathy built the chain on Biblical principles and a high attention to customer service. Workers often circulate the restaurant floor to attend to customer needs. At the end of each transaction, the restaurant workers say, "It's my pleasure." By choice, it's the only fast food chain to be closed on Sundays. Among his top ten tips for entrepreneurial success, Cathy says, "Be kind to people. Courtesy is very cheap but brings great dividends." Chick-fil-A is a clear example of branding being more than just a logo or marketing campaign.

The Walt Disney Company has established a ubiquitous brand. According to the Disney Institute, an arm of the company that teaches its principles, Disney credits its success to the powerful link between guest satisfaction and brand reputation. Disney trains its employees to create "magical moments" for its customers that keep them coming back. "If we focused on big 'wow' moments, can we maintain it on a daily basis? Absolutely not!" Disney Institute facilitator Nicole Lauria said. "We must do these little things too. Never underestimate the power of what seems like small initiatives."

## Questions for Reflection

1. Do you have a marketing plan? How do you know if it is working?

_____

_____

_____

_____

2. Do you have a unique brand? What does it stand for?

_____

_____

_____

_____

3. What makes your brand different than your top three competitors?

_____

_____

_____

_____

## Chapter Five

## Be Giving

"Make all you can, save all you can, give all you can."

~ John Wesley

Each Christmas, the law firm of Minor and Brown in Denver, Colorado gives each employee twenty one-dollar bills. The workers then fan out across the city, finding organizations and people who can use the money to make a difference, even if it's a small one.

Across the country, Target Corporation gives out $500 million a year to support education and literacy. The Target CEO says the company has always believed in strengthening the communities in which it does business.

Big or small, corporations drive much of the philanthropy in this country. Philanthropy is a big word, but even the smallest businesses can participate in it. Most companies find a way to give: 91 percent of small businesses give to charity, and 83 percent also give through volunteering their time, according to the Better Business Bureau. Perhaps some give only for the tax break or to generate good publicity; however, for many entrepreneurs, the thrill of success really comes from being able to use their resources for something greater than themselves.

At McAfee, a giving spirit is part of our culture. We approach philanthropy in a variety of ways. It is driven by a selfless attitude in how we approach every job, in giving financially to organizations and individuals through our foundation (which I'll explain later), and in the way we share our time to help others. We've been giving since the first year of business, when my wife and I sponsored a Little League team. We loved going to their games! When the season ended, we took the team out for ice cream. It was really a simple gesture, but it was an important start in what would become a principle of business that I believe has helped carry us to this level of success. The dream is much more than a "me" thing. It's not about how much we can make, but about who we can help along the way. We're focused on our responsibility to help meet the needs of those around us, children in particular. A question we ask frequently is, "How can we help someone experience something they couldn't otherwise experience on their own?"

## Creating a Culture of Selflessness

Most people assume giving starts with a check written to charity or with a few hours of volunteer time. In a company, though, it really starts with the standards you set for how you treat your customers and employees. Giving should start at home. We pay our people well and provide good benefits. I've extended no-interest loans to employees caught in tough situations and allow them to pay us back over time. Seeing employees build solid lives for their families motivates me to carry on with my dream. It continues to remind me that it's not all about me — that the dreams of my employees are interwoven with their work at my company.

A selfless culture also extends into the homes we service. We spend thousands of dollars each year on shoe protectors to wear inside clients' homes. Why? Certainly not because it's a good policy or impressive, but because we truly care about the homes we step foot in and want to show respect to the people who live there — the customers who are gracious enough to give us their business. Because we value our customers' time and schedule, we call ahead before we arrive at an appointment and make sure to be on time. If we happen to underestimate on a price quote, we honor our original estimate, despite the loss.

It will be difficult to engage your employees in meaningful charity work if they feel the company doesn't respect them or clients. When you set a high standard of caring for employees and clients, they are more likely to share your enthusiasm for helping others. I know that if I weren't here, McAfee would still be a giving company because of the standards we've engrained into our culture.

**Why Be Generous?**

One calling of mine happens to be giving. It's become part of who I am as a person, and that extends into my life as a business owner. I find giving to be both fulfilling and rewarding, even though that is not why I give in the first place. You shouldn't give just to see what you can get back in return, but the blessing of giving is that it always seems to come back to you many times over in some form.

While I believe philanthropy is a corporate responsibility, telling other entrepreneurs to give away precious profits because it is the right thing to do can be a hard sell. So let's take a look at the business case for giving. A recent report from the Committee for Encouraging Corporate Philanthropy gives insight into research-backed reasons for corporate giving:

**Company giving enhances employee engagement.**

Employees are more motivated and loyal to a company

when they feel engaged through group volunteer programs

and know about their company's philanthropy. It provides

a sense of identification with the organization.

VARtek, an education software company located in Dayton, Ohio, engaged its employees in charitable giving by having them rank a diverse list of charities that the company was considering giving to during the holiday season. The company gave $1,000 donations to the top four, as chosen by the staff, and the employees felt proud to be part of the company's efforts.

**Company giving builds customer loyalty.** According to

the report, a company's commitment to communities and

certain philanthropic causes enhanced brand perception,

customer loyalty, repeat business, and word-of-mouth promotion.

**Company giving contributes to business innovation and growth opportunities.** Philanthropy also gives businesses new relationships and opportunities to test, demonstrate new ideas, technologies and products.

Another study, conducted in 2004 by Deloitte LLP highlights another benefit: stronger recruitment. A company's philanthropic initiatives can set it apart for a job candidate. Deloitte researchers found that 72 percent of employed Americans trying to decide between a job where everything else — location, job description, pay, and benefits — was equal would choose the company that also supports charitable causes.

**Giving Financially: Make a Plan**

It's important, even as a small business, to manage your giving professionally. Philanthropy should be part of your strategic planning. During your planning, consider some important questions that will help guide your giving:

- What kinds of causes do we feel most passionately about? What aligns with our business?

- How much should we give of our profits annually? On average, small businesses give 6 percent of net profits annually to charity, according to an American Express study.

- Should we give through a foundation? Should we manage the foundation ourselves or use an outside firm such as an accountant, attorney, or community foundation that offers services for donor-directed funds?

- How will we research individuals and organizations making requests? You can review nonprofit financial statements at Guidestar.org and charitynavigator.org.

- Will we seek or accept publicity for our donations?

- How will we communicate with our employees about our giving? In meetings or through in-house newsletters? Will they be asked to give? How?

- Will we participate in community fundraising campaigns such as United Way?

Reviewing these types of issues in advance can help make giving a joyful experience instead of a burden. It will set a framework for giving that can grow with your company.

## How It Has Worked for Them

Jim Bowman, chief executive officer of RexArc International Inc., says his company makes sure the values of the charitable organization dovetail with the corporate values of the company. "Be proactive and target a few charitable organizations in advance and at the annual budgeting process for the next fiscal year rather than just using the first-come/first-served approach and making a knee-jerk promise at an emotional point to a phone solicitation," he said.

## Why We Started a Foundation

From the beginning, McAfee has given to a variety of organizations. Part of our strategic planning included giving to a local organization that aligned with our mission of improving air quality and helping youth. After several years in business, we decided to start The

McAfee Foundation for Children and Youth to focus our giving on

children's causes. This made our processes more professional and gave us

a formal way to solicit donations from our employees (through a payroll

deduction), as well as from our customers, who are offered a chance to

give $100 to the foundation in return for a high-efficiency air cleaner.

The Foundation supports individuals, as well as groups. About 80

percent of our giving goes to the Children's Medical Center of Dayton. A

few years ago, in our desire to support a local organization dedicated to

children and clean indoor air; we began a partnership with the hospital

Pulmonary Department. The hospital uses our donations to purchase

supplies such as inhalers, to help parents with the cost of gas to get to and

from the hospital, or to help cover insurance co-pays for families who are

struggling to afford medical care for their children. The hospital also refers

families to us who need to create a cleaner air environment for their

children, who might be suffering from ailments like lung cancer or severe

allergies. We have donated air duct cleanings and high-efficiency air

cleaners, assessed heating and cooling systems, and added special filters.

One of the most moving experiences in my life as a business

owner came through a random opportunity to give to a family in need. It

was close to Christmas, and my wife happened to hear of a local woman who was taking in four children from an abusive situation in a neighboring state. When she told me the heart-wrenching story, I knew we had to do something to help. The children had experienced every type of abuse imaginable, as well as things no one would ever want to imagine happening to any child. We took the story to our staff, and they rallied to help. Through the generosity of our employees, the foster mom was able to provide new clothes, supplies, and toys for the kids that Christmas. She shared with us:

> I had the pleasure of working with Mr. McAfee through his generous Children's and Youth Program during the winter of 2007. He helped orchestrate an outreach plan for four new foster children. Greg put this idea into action and continues to do so for other children through his Foundation. He is not only touching the lives of children he has never met, but also really changing sorrowful situations for many children who would be at a disadvantage otherwise.

I mention this not to boast. In actuality, what we were able to provide for the family was minor compared to the overall needs of those children. Nevertheless, it was a special experience because we quickly mobilized for something more important than the daily grind of running a business. We were able to use our power to respond when we felt called to do so.

When you build a team of people who care about people and a business that has the resources to give, you can experience the joy of giving to others in crisis.

**Donating Time**

Even when economic times are tough, you don't have to put giving opportunities on the back burner. If your ability to donate financially declines, I challenge you to be creative in your philanthropy. There's no reason it can't continue, even if by different means. In fact, it could be a great elixir for low morale during difficult times. Often, the magnitude of your own problems shrinks in light of the hardships others are facing. Viktor E. Frankl, Holocaust survivor and author of the 1946 book *Man's Search for Meaning*, shared that the concentration camp survivors who tried to give purpose to their days by helping others were more likely to survive.

We've found several ways to give in addition to financial donations. The staff recently collected old cell phones for an organization that distributes them to battered women, who can use them to call 911 in an emergency. Some nonprofits need your time and expertise as much as they need monetary donations. Are there nonprofits that can use you on their board? What about schools who need tutors or speakers? Look for community-wide days of service to find easy opportunities to plug in and make a difference.

**Dreaming Beyond Yourself**

Many people think a business should grow and prosper and give back later. I did the opposite: I grew and gave at the same time. If you make giving part of your culture from the very beginning, it will be easier to continue giving along the way.

I challenge you, wherever you are financially, to find a way for your business to impact the community around you. Giving will propel your dream into something much bigger than yourself. When you are able to help someone accomplish something they couldn't do on their own, it can give wings to their dreams too. Start giving today and make an impact on someone's life.

## Questions for Reflection

1. What percent of your annual budget do you give to charity and why?

_____

_____

_____

_____

2. How do you make "giving" decisions? Is it part of your strategic

planning?

_____

_____

_____

_____

3. What issues are you most passionate about?

_____

_____

_____

_____

4. How can these become part of your strategic giving plan?

_____

_____

_____

_____

**Chapter Six**

**Be Innovative**

"Innovation distinguishes between a leader and a follower."

~ Steve Jobs

America has flourished through innovation, built upon the hard

work and creativity of inventors and entrepreneurs. In Dayton, Ohio,

where I live and work, it's hard not to be inspired by the history of

innovation in this slice of the country alone. Dayton inventors pioneered

the cash register, the yo-yo, the electric car starter, the ring-pull can, the

Boolean search method, and of course, human flight, at the innovative

minds and hands of Orville and Wilbur Wright.

You might think, *But I'm just a small business owner installing air*

*conditioners and fixing furnaces. How innovative can I be?* Let me assure

you that innovation is the key to surviving! *Innovation* simply means

coming up with new and better ways of doing something. It means taking

an old way of thinking — even something as simple as how you schedule

your appointments — and figuring out how to do it better. What a thrill it is to see an innovative idea take off and work! Innovation is worth the risk of failing, worth the risk that comes with being first to bring an idea to market. Staying in the *status quo* might feel safe, but in the long term, that's the truly risky way to run a business.

## Being First to Market

In our attempts to be innovative, we've made lots of mistakes. We've had to adjust, tinker, and sometimes just throw out entire ideas. But we keep trying.

We've had some major wins. If we didn't have an innovative spirit and willingness to be first in our market to try new things, we would never have made the leap from a tiny startup to a thriving, growing business. There are several advantages to being first to enter the market, and the chief among them are consumer impact and lack of competition.

We experienced both when we took the risk of launching after-hours service. If you've ever had to have a service person come to your home — whether it was for plumbing or cable TV hookup — you know that no one in our market was working late hours. We set a new level of expectation for consumers: They know we are willing and able to meet their schedules while other companies are not. Some other firms have tried, but none have branded it in the way we have. Consumers were eager to have a heating and air service company that would accommodate their schedules without them having to miss valuable earning hours at their jobs. Being first means you can set expectations for your industry that others then have to scramble to reach. Our "8:00 to 8:00 at the Same Great Rate!" promotion drives much of our new business. It continues to strengthen our brand, giving us name recognition and exclusivity.

Companies that are first to market earn themselves at least a short-term hold by being first. If they do it well, they will be able to maintain a leading presence when their competition enters the market.

It is critical to take full advantage of that head start, for the risks of being first to market can sting. You must do it well enough to keep the consumers' loyalty when the market floods with competition — and it will!

Market pioneers must overcome several obstacles that their followers will not have to face. For one, they face market ignorance. Even armed with the best research, it's difficult to know just how consumers will react to a truly innovative idea. The companies who follow can, on the other hand, base their moves on actual, proven consumer reaction. The first to enter also takes on a considerably higher cost of innovation and must worry about cheaper knockoffs.

Despite the risks, I still push my company to be first to market with new ideas, and I encourage you to do the same. We took a risk for innovation about eight years ago when we decided to private label our own HVAC systems. For twelve years, we had installed a well-recognized brand name. In fact, we marketed the brand so well that customers thought we were them. For years, we toyed with the idea of putting our own private label on the units we installed, and finally, we partnered with a manufacturer to private label our McAfee system. At first, we installed our units *and* the other brand, but this quickly became too confusing for our customers, and they began to question, "Hmm. Which one is better?" When we realized we were, in essence, competing with ourselves, we decided to embrace the private label and exclusively brand it as a high-end unit. People already trusted our name, and now they could trust the product with our name on it. Others who have tried to private label often approach theirs as a less expensive line, while we set out to make ours the best, and the proof is in the pudding: We have grown every year since we began private labeling.

I often share the story of Mary M., a customer during the time we started private labeling. Mary read an article in the local newspaper about our venture to private label, after we were scheduled to install one of the other brand units in her home that week. She called that morning and asked how much more it would cost to install a McAfee system. We knew right then that our plan was going to work.

Trying to dominate your market instead of simply duplicating those in the lead makes coming to work every day exciting. Ask yourself if you want to be a leader. If that answer is "YES!" then go for it!


**Fostering a Culture of Innovation**

Innovation absolutely must be part of your company's culture. As the leader, it's up to you to set the stage for a sense of adventure and freedom to encourage employees to develop and share new ideas.

As we've grown, we have been intentional with the interior design of our offices to encourage creativity. Many HVAC offices are dark and outdated — some downright scary! Here, we emphasize a clean, bright, welcoming atmosphere. We choose to invest in modern amenities to set a certain image and tone for our staff, vendors, and customers who walk through our door. Details matter: Adequate and nicely appointed bathrooms, a bright break room where employees can truly get away, and televisions throughout the facility give our working environment a creative boost.

We created our own "Dream Room" concept with sky-blue walls, red chairs, black leather couches, and even a wild, bright carpet. The atmosphere puts us in a place to dream and think and be more innovative.

In our sheet metal shop, we upgraded to brighter (and more expensive) lamps that replicate outdoor lighting. It costs us more each month, but it is worth the expense to boost productivity by providing a well-lit workspace. Employees want to come to work each day in a fun, modern environment. If you want to hire high-caliber people, you have to offer a high-caliber atmosphere.

Your operations are also a great place to be innovative. We make it a point to have as much up-to-date equipment as we can justify, including our phone systems and real-time scheduling software. We invest in training so our staff will learn the latest methods of being more efficient. These investments improve our bottom line because they equip our people to be more productive in a better environment.

Whether you are situated in a garage, a small building, or a skyscraper, you set the standards of your company atmosphere. Even a one-man shop can have the right equipment, and the right equipment will pay for itself quickly. When we worked out of the garage, we were innovative. For instance, we chose to deliver everything for free. Why? Because we didn't want customers to see that we were smaller than they thought. Even still, the garage was very clean and looked like an office. You can be innovative at any stage of business, but we have never been so innovative that it didn't make sense. When laptops were $3,000, we didn't go out and buy one for every truck. Now that they have come down in price, it makes more sense. If you do the best you can afford, you can still be innovative. I sometimes hear owners of small shops say, "We turn down new customers all the time because we can't get to them." When I hear that, I cringe. Surely they can — and must — find a way! I have no problem spending money to attract new customers, and there is no way I am going to turn any potential clients away.

To be innovative, you have to be willing to move beyond the way it's always been. According to the late Ronald Reagan, "*Status quo*, you know, that is Latin for 'the mess we're in.'" We long held to the idea of making sure a live person answered every incoming call on or before the second ring. In fact, it was a hard and fast rule of our office. However, we recently hired a full-time operator who dispatches the calls, and it became clear that it simply is not possible for her to answer the frequent calls within two rings. To implement a new, more effective system, I had to be willing to let go of the old rule. Now, we answer within four rings. Nothing is written in stone, and you must be willing to change if it is for a good reason.

To take that idea further, an innovator has to rid a business of people who aren't willing to work and change within the environment. At McAfee, if a new employee appears to be a bad fit, we let them go within the first ninety days, and we make every effort to be honest with them and part as friends. An innovator must be okay with moving people out — for the good of the company and for the good of the poorly fitting employee. I have hired several salespeople who didn't work out for us, but I kept right on hiring until we found the right ones. We've hired and fired many people to find those who fit our culture, and I have now clenched the concept of hiring slow, firing fast!

An innovative person has to embrace failure. Don't be afraid of change: It's the key to innovation and seeing your dream come true!

## Questions for Reflection

1. Name one area of your company in which you can be innovative. Then, make a plan to make the necessary changes.

_____

_____

_____

_____

2. Do your employees feel they have the freedom to make suggestions for innovation? Ask them why or why not.

_____

_____

_____

_____

3. When was the last time you made any significant changes in your company?

_____

_____

_____

_____

## Chapter Seven

## Be Passionate

"Without passion, you don't have energy;
without energy, you have nothing."

~ Donald Trump

Your relationship with your business isn't that different from a

marriage. Every aspect is an adventure during the startup (dating) phase.

You are passionate and energetic, and you want to come to work, like a

suitor clamoring for the next date. Like marriage, the business's success,

as well as your own contentment, will ultimately rest upon how well you

can maintain that high level of passion. During challenging times, keeping

a passionate and driven attitude can largely determine whether your

business survives or fails. Passion is what powers you through the grunt

work, the long hours, and all those inherent risks. Passion drives you to

keep coming back, trying new things, and launching new ideas.

Conversely, like a passionless marriage, a passionless business venture is

miserable for all involved. Some scholars have denigrated passion as

clouding reason; they pit passion and reason against one another, with reason the superior choice. But research published in the *Academy of Management Review* suggests that entrepreneurial passion actually can be a driving force in success. Passion can help entrepreneurs creatively solve problems, identify new opportunities, and master challenging situations.

I've found this to be true in my business. As the owner, I set the pace for passion. At times, I've been mistaken for being upset when I have been really excited over something in the business. I have always been passionate about things I am interested in. As a young boy delivering newspapers, I was passionate about my route. It was such a good feeling to get all the papers delivered on time. Entrepreneurial passion isn't something that comes about because entrepreneurs are inherently disposed to it. Rather, it's because they are engaged in something they love and can relate to well. Michael Dell, founder and CEO of Dell, Inc., said, "Passion should be the fire that drives your life's work." Does your dream fit that description? Is it meaningful to you? It's difficult to stay passionate about something that isn't in your heart, such as a family business you never wanted to lead or a venture that seems profitable but terribly boring. Your dream must be your passion.

Staying passionate about your business is easier when you identify the areas you care most about. For me, that's been serving others, growth, and finishing well. Henry Ford quipped, "I do not believe a man can ever leave his business. He ought to think of it by day and dream of it by night."

## Passionate About Growth

I knew from early on that I didn't want to be a one-man shop. I was passionate about growing a heating and air company, even before I knew much about business. Of course, passion alone was not what caused customers to start calling, but entrepreneurial passion did give me the energy to pursue growth opportunities, invest in marketing, and continually strive for improvement.

As I completed goals, my passion grew for the little things that would have big bottom-line results, such as improving our hiring and scheduling processes. I'm passionate about reaching a certain sales goal, how many trucks we'll have someday, what our facilities will look like in the future, and how many people we will employ. I thrive on envisioning what growth will look like for my company, what the McAfee of 2020 and beyond will be.

Passion is contagious: When someone is passionate, they attract others. Therefore, your passion will motivate your staff. Help your team set goals that tie directly to the growth of the business and celebrate their victories. "Winning is a habit. Unfortunately, so is losing," said Vince Lombardi.

We were very passionate about making our "8:00 to 8:00 at the Same Great Rate" promotion work. As soon as the idea came up, we were passionate about making it happen. The growth that has come from launching that new schedule motivated us to continue and to persevere in trying other novel concepts in our market.

How do you stay passionate if your business isn't growing? Don't get overwhelmed! Find something you just love about it. Even when you aren't growing, you can strive to do things well. Everyone gets into a slump now and then, regardless of what business you are in, but you simply have to keep looking ahead and expecting growth. We all have our valleys to cross and mountains to go over. More businesses fail going up the mountain than down; you just have to be prepared to handle the growth and plan accordingly.

Passionate people rarely give up; however, they do have to know when to put a bad idea to sleep or make serious changes and adjustments. One thing you should never cut back on, though, is your will to be stronger and better than before.

In *Today Matters*, John C. Maxwell writes, "For years I kept a sign on my desk that helped me maintain the right perspective concerning yesterday. It simply said, 'Yesterday ended last night.' It reminds me that no matter how badly I might have failed in the past, it's done, and today is a new day. Conversely, no matter what goals I may have accomplished or awards I may have received, they have little direct impact on what I do today. I can't celebrate my way to success either." I take that to mean this: Success or failure, we should not get stuck in the muck of either. We must keep moving!

Being passionate about growth will keep you from becoming satisfied. The worst thing for a business owner to do is to become complacent. By definition, complacency deals with being self-satisfied with your accomplishments while being unaware of potential danger. It's like the contractor who worked years to dominate his market. Until he reached the top, he was motivated to risk more, work overtime, take business classes, and do whatever he needed to do to reach his goal. When he finally hit that pinnacle, he was overwhelmed with a sense of accomplishment and self-satisfaction. Riding the waves of all he had learned and accomplished, he did a great job for a while, but he never learned about professional management, and he did nothing to keep his business running without him. He rode that wave way too long and became satisfied. Eventually, the competition, which remained very hungry, caught up with him and surpassed him, finally putting his company out of business.

If we are not careful, we can allow our accomplishments, victories, and knowledge to cause us to become satisfied in our current stage of achievement. When you do experience periods of fast growth, it can threaten your passion. Owners often don't know how to handle growth, and business becomes more of a hassle rather than an opportunity. When this happens, you will be more likely to hire employees too quickly and neglect properly training them. This will ultimately hurt your service and affect your business culture, if you allow it to. It can also squelch new employees' own passion when they can't perform well because they don't know the expectations or haven't been properly trained to do the tasks they are called to do.

It's critical for business owners to control their growth; just because you have a big job opportunity doesn't mean you should take it. Be wise!

## Passionate About Service

One of the hallmarks of our business is our passion for customer service. Angie Downey, my current executive assistant, is one of the best customer service representatives I have ever met. She has a unique way of making the customer think ideas and solutions are their own. She eagerly and efficiently trains new CSRs and handles the most difficult issues that might arise.

Our sense of urgency has separated us from the competition. I've never been the most patient person, so I've taken that weakness and turned it into strength for my business. We get to the customer as quickly as possible because I, myself, do not like to wait. We train our installers to complete installations within one day because I do not like workers in my house for long periods of time. We train our CSRs in proper phone etiquette so customers will sense that their service call is the most important call of the day. Customer service keeps our customers coming back and referring us to others, so we consider it a critical ingredient to our longevity. After all, what is a customer service business if they don't service customers properly?

Being passionate about service must radiate from you to your entire staff. In seasonal businesses like heating and air, it's not easy to maintain the same high level of passion year round. During the slower times, our service technicians and installers tend to get comfortable working shorter shifts. Perhaps more importantly, so do their families. About three weeks before the busy season begins, we start to gear up. We meet with our service techs and installers, prepping them for the changes and explaining why we push so hard during our busy season.

I have sent letters home to forewarn families when the busy season is approaching. Once our staff begins working longer hours, we arrange for little perks, such as providing Gatorade to workers out in the field or gift cards for a local ice cream shop that they can take home to their families. It is a challenge to keep up morale in the busiest times, but as a leader — a coach — it is my job to rally the troops and prepare them for what lies ahead. In the past, I would wait until several days into the season to give a pep talk, but I learned that by then, the message was reactive and no longer proactive. I have set a more positive tone by approaching it early and sharing my own passion for the small window of opportunity our company has each summer and winter to make the bulk of our revenue.

Hiring passionate employees is also critical when it comes to maintaining our level of customer service. How can you detect true passion? Most people can feign enthusiasm in interviews, especially when they really want and need the job. When I'm interviewing potential

employees, I like to ask about their hobbies. Listening to someone describe

what they voluntarily put their time and effort into doing — rebuilding

engines, cultivating a garden, exercising — reveals their capacity for

passion. A person who cares about nothing in their personal life is likely to

care about little at work.

---

### An Important Lesson in Customer Service

Early in our business, we sold a system to Vito U., the general manager of a local cafeteria. I told him we would arrive at his home at eight a.m. for his installation. For some odd reason, we were running late and arrived at eight fifteen. I knocked on his door and received no answer, so I assume he wasn't home.

Seconds later, he appeared at the door and greeted me with a cold stare and a warning: "If you were in the restaurant business, you would be out of business."

"Excuse me?" I said.

He continued, "In order for us to open at eight, we have to come in at five. I guess I just expected you here on time."

I was taken aback by his actions and remarks, but I never forgot his words. From that point on, we guaranteed that our first appointment of the day–and any other appointments we could control–would begin on time, right down to the minute. I realized how important that was for him, and for every customer. We don't arrive early or late. Arriving ten minutes early can throw off the schedule of a parent getting kids ready for school. You have to be on time, plain and simple. I had always been concerned about being on time for a job, but until that moment, I didn't realize how important it was to be there at exactly the right time. It became an important principle of our business, and we do not waver from it today.

## Passionate About Finishing Well

Projects left unfinished are a burden upon shoulders. Isn't that an awful feeling, a disappointment in yourself for leaving something hanging? An unfinished project can zap energy and passion if you're not vigorous about completing it. Within the company, one thing we take very seriously is finishing well. We have a goal to finish an installation in one day, which is faster than our market standard. Setting those goals drives the passion to make it happen. When our installation crew arrives on a job, they quickly design a system to meet their goal. Every job is different, from the layout of the home, to the layout of the system, to the amount of preparation needed. Our attention to completing each job to its own specifications and in a timely manner ties directly to revenue and customer satisfaction. With an installation, we have one shot to make an impression on our customer since we aren't likely to be back for a year or two.

When we bring in new installers who have previous experience from other companies, they first wonder how installing in one day is possible, but with training they, too, adapt to our way. Once this is mastered, the next step is to become faster and more efficient. I'll admit that we do operate most tasks around here at a fast pace. There is an installation timeline, and we hold our teams accountable for meeting those times: when an existing system is removed, what time the duct work is ordered, when the outside unit is completed, and what time the indoor unit is set and ready to hook up. It's the "McAfee Way" of installing, and it works well for us and allows our jobs to flow well.

Personally, I am passionate about successfully finishing well the goals before me. I don't want to let my advisory board or my team down.

In fact, having an advisory board and leadership team helps me remain passionate about pushing through the difficult steps to the finish line.

## Rekindling Passion

As I've mentioned, we all have mountaintop and valley experiences in our lives and in our businesses. At some point, our passion can falter under the pressure of running a business. Perhaps you grew too fast and couldn't keep up with the changes, or maybe business has slowed and the harsh realities of layoffs and cutbacks have left you depressed. Maybe something in your personal life is draining your motivation or you just can't keep up with everyone on your agenda. You are still dedicated to your dream, but the passion that drove the will to succeed has waned. It's okay! Know that there is hope to rekindle and sustain passion in your business.

There are owners who say they are content to run small shops with minimal growth, but in my own experience, I've come to realize that many of the people at that level can be just as stressed as someone running a large company. Without the resources of a team, there is only so much one or two people can do. For many, running a one-man show or a mom-and-pop shop becomes a twenty-four/seven endeavor, leading to burnout, and the passion to make their business work quickly fades. Running a business

leaves them in a dreary, overworked routine with little to show for it. If

this sounds familiar, consider making a concentrated effort to become

more passionate about your business. Surround yourself with passionate

people. Read books by passionate authors such as John C. Maxwell, Ken

Blanchard, Jim Collins, or Jeffery Gitomer. Identify what stresses you the

most in your business and set out to eliminate it. What brings you joy and

happiness in business? Whatever it is, figure out a way to do more of it.

Many business owners go through what I call a "moping period."

Don't worry, for so does the American bald eagle. At a certain age, the

bald eagle goes through a depressing state of life. Their feathers get thick

and ruffled, their beaks build up hard calcium, and their talons become

dull. Eagle experts will even tell you that the majestic bird may lose its

will to live. As is the case with so much in nature, though, an amazing

thing happens: Other eagles stop by and drop fresh meat down to the

depressed eagle, squawking encouragements to them to eat, take to the

sky, and renew themselves. Like the eagle, many business owners go

through a similar "moping period." They lose their drive and passion to be

in business. When profit is low and debts are high, it can take a toll on an

individual, draining the zest they once had for the business they have strived to build. They mistakenly think if they just make it go away, they'll feel better, and they begin to doubt if they should be in business at all. One of my favorite Bible verses, Isaiah 40:31 (KJV), proclaims, "But they that wait upon the LORD shall renew their strength; they shall mount up with wings as eagles; they shall run, and not be weary; and they shall walk, and not faint." My friend, I hope this book can be the fresh meat you need to take to the sky with your business again! There are five ways to avoid the moping period:

1. Set realistic goals.

2. Don't spend more than you make.

3. Keep changing and improving.

4. Avoid getting neither satisfied nor comfortable.

5. Hang around other eagles (not chickens).


At McAfee, it seems we're constantly changing in an effort to improve and grow. This could entail adding a new vanity phone number, a new procedure, a uniform change, a new logo, a new technology, or a new system — any new and better way of doing something. Looking to the future drives me, and it can drive you, but you have to dream about it. It would be very hard for me to keep my passion up if I came into work and did the same thing every single day. Think about a changeup pitch in

baseball. The changeup is thrown with the same arm action as a fastball,

but at a lower velocity due to the pitcher holding the ball in a special grip.

Longtime pitching coach Leo Mazzone explains in his book, *Pitch Like a*

*Pro:*

> When a pitcher throws his best fastball, he puts more in it;
>
> the changeup is such that one throws something other than
>
> his best fastball. By having this mindset, the pitch will
>
> have less velocity on it in addition to the change in grips.
>
> This difference from what is expected by the arm action
>
> and the velocity can confuse the batter into swinging the
>
> bat far too early and thus receiving a strike, or not
>
> swinging at all. Should a batter be fooled on the timing of
>
> the pitch and still make contact, it will cause a foul ball or
>
> the ball being put into play weakly, usually resulting in an
>
> out. In addition to the unexpected slow velocity, the
>
> changeup can also possess a significant amount of
>
> movement, which can bewilder the batter even further.
>
> The very best changeups utilize both deception and
>
> movement.

If the pitcher threw a fastball every time, the batter would know what to expect and get more hits, and perhaps even more noteworthy, the pitcher wouldn't last long. He would throw his arm out and have to retire young! How does this relate to business? Simply put, don't get satisfied, change things up every so often, and make it fun!

I also challenge you to consider what other areas of your business excite you the most. If you can't think of any, you might need to ask yourself some bigger questions: *Is this really my dream? Is this truly my passion or just something I fell into? Why am I doing this?* If you're not passionate about your dream, you're probably not going to be passionate about making it happen.

**Questions for Reflection**

1. What is your passion? Take some time to reflect on what you are most passionate about in life and within your business. How can you spend more time on those things?

---

---

---

---

2. How do you sustain passion in your business? Among your employees?

_____

_____

_____

_____

## Chapter Eight

## Be Ready

"Before everything else, getting ready is the secret of success."

~ Henry Ford

If you implement the principles in this book, your personal and business lives are going to change. I'm convinced that if you follow these eight steps, your business will grow and prosper: Be strategic, be teachable, be a coach, be known, be giving, be innovative, be passionate, and be ready. It's a potent combination for success! I've experienced it, and I hope you will too. That's why I want to encourage you to be ready. "Ready for what?" you ask. Be ready for growth and for an incredible ride. If you forge ahead with these principles, be prepared for change to come about.

Let's review:

**Be strategic.** No dream — no matter how small or audacious — will come to life without a strategy. Find time to dream and plan, get the right people at the table to help you, and continually update and refer to your plan to stay on track for your dream.

**Be teachable.** To grow as a leader, you must be teachable. Read the best books, take classes, and spend time with business leaders who have grown their businesses.

Most important, put together a board of competent, wise, capable, and trustworthy advisors for your business. The advice you receive and the accountability they provide is priceless.

**Be a coach.** Are you a manager or a coach? Coaches step back and see the entire field, empowering others on their team to lead and work in their own ways while still carrying out the team's values and mission.

**Be known.** Spending money on advertising, branding, and marketing is a necessary risk if you want to lead in your market. If someone is going to use your service, they've got to know your name.

**Be giving.** Aside from just being the right thing to do, building a giving culture in your business can have many practical benefits, such as employee engagement, stronger brand perception, and customer loyalty.

**Be innovative.** Innovation simply means coming up with new and better ways of doing something. How long have you done the same old thing day after day? Better yet, do you let the people you hire try new things or think new thoughts?

**Be passionate.** Before you can be motivated; you must have
passion! It's the fuel that inspires us to act and it makes life worth living.
Our passion is about who we are; our dreams are about what we want to
become.

## And Now, We Must Be Ready

More than twenty years ago, I took the huge risk of leaving the
kind of life I knew to follow my dream of being a business owner. With
the right approach, our growth (which came in swift order at times) didn't
catch us off guard. We were ready and able to ride each step to the next
level.

You might be sitting in your garage or in your home office
wondering if growth can really come to a small business in America today.
It can! Just think: It wasn't long ago that my wife and I sat at our humble
kitchen table to pay the company bills! It wasn't long ago that I was
staring at my backyard, strategizing where I'd build a bigger garage. It
wasn't long ago I was sitting across from an empty lot, dreaming of the
corporate headquarters we would someday build. It wasn't but a few
months ago, while writing this book, that I dreamed of renovating my
entire building and making it more employee and customer friendly. We

have created a strong small business by implementing the principles I've

shared in this book. If I can do it, so can you! In fact, your biggest concern

shouldn't be *whether* you can grow, but how to handle it when you *do*.

The best way to manage growth is to go back to the first principle

of this book: Be strategic. You'll need a strong plan — one that includes

specifics about what your business will need to look like to move to the

next level of revenue.

Be ready to risk more. You have to risk more capital to hire more

people, to buy bigger buildings, to buy more trucks, and to buy more

equipment. Risk is where the rubber meets the road, and it scares some

people to death. Those kinds of people would rather stay a small company,

but for many entrepreneurs, me included, this is where it gets fun. Even

though some might say it's less risky as you gain experience, calculated

risks still give me the rush that I thrive on.

Be ready to spend your time wisely. Have a plan for your time.

Mine is spent on growing my business and looking to the future. As you

grow, revisit the chapter on coaching. You'll need to continually ask

yourself what others can be doing so you can focus your time doing

whatever it is that only you can do. In other words, if someone else can do

a certain task, they should be tasked with it. Be ready for the freedom to do what you do best — that should be dreaming and growing the business. As my friend and Aileron instructor Dave S. says, "An entrepreneur should be employed from the neck up." Keep your hands off your business and use your mind to think and dream.

Be ready for the next dream. I'm never satisfied and am always looking for the next challenge. For now, I'm continually pushing to remain to be a market leader and finding ways to help other entrepreneurs grow, which is why I wrote this book. What's your next dream? I remember driving to Dayton Firestone as a 19-year-old, thinking I was heading for the best opportunity of my life. I couldn't have guessed how the next twenty years of my life would unfold. I've learned how to visualize a dream and go after it, and I can't wait to hear how you are doing the same.

Please contact me at **dreamer@gregmcafee.com** to share your story...

**It's ~~My~~ Your Dream!**

## The Open Book
## Game of Business

# TRAIN YOUR HVAC TEAM
## WITH THE OPEN BOOK GAME OF BUSINESS: TOBGOB

TOBGOB® is an innovative board game that HVAC entrepreneurs use to teach their teams how to act like an entrepreneur and boost productivity in the process. Through four rounds of play, you have the opportunity to introduce the principles of "open book management" to your HVAC business. TOBGOB is a great way for individuals or teams to build camaraderie and ownership.

Think of how much fun you had playing games while you were growing up. Nothing helps bring a group into new awareness and connectedness like a board game. TOBGOB acts as a creativity exercise for educational intervention. It makes learning fun and accessible! The objective of TOBGOB is to help HVAC staff members understand how their actions affect the financial success of the company.

**Order today at www.tobgob.com**

# A MARKETING PLAN THAT SETS YOUR HVAC BUSINESS APART

More than a memorable phone number, 1-800-AIR-REPAIR can be a marketing cornerstone for your heating, air conditioning, or air duct cleaning business. Based on a subscription, the vanity number is exclusively assigned to geographic marketing areas in the United States. Leads and sales calls from your area code are routed directly to you, 24 hours a day, 7 days a week, 365 days a year.

With our exclusive marketing support system and your investment of time, your business can grow to exceed your expectations, and you can make your dream of a successful, profitable organization a reality. Don't wait... and don't miss another opportunity for a sale. Reserve your area code now at **www.1-800-air-repair.com**

## Resources and Works Cited

Aileron. http://www.aileron.org/.

Allen, Scott. "Henry Ford: Founder of Ford Motor Company and Assembly

Line Innovator."

http://entrepreneurs.about.com/od/famousentrepreneurs/p/henryfor

d.htm.

American Marketing Association. "Definition of Marketing."

http://www.marketingpower.com/AboutAMA/Pages/Definitionof

Marketing.aspx.

Better Business Bureau. "Small Business Charitable Giving Guide for the

Holiday Season." 31 October 2007.

http://www.bbb.org/us/article/small-business-charitable-giving-

guide-for-the-holiday-season-1907.

"Black and Decker Dustbuster." Wikipedia, modified 11 March 2011.

http://en.wikipedia.org/wiki/Black_%26_Decker_DustBuster.

Black and Decker. http://www.blackanddecker.com/.

Blanchard, Ken, The Ken Blanchard Companies.

http://www.kenblanchard.com/.

Bowman, Jim, RexArc International, Inc. http://www.rexarc.com/.

Burkett, Larry. *Business by the Book.* Thomas Nelson Publishers, 2003.

Cardon, M.S.; J. Wincent; J. Singh; and M. Drnovsek. "The Nature and

Experience of Entrepreneurial Passion." *Academy of Management*

*Review*, 2009.

"Changeup." Wikipedia, modified 17 September 2011.

http://en.wikipedia.org/wiki/Changeup.

Chick-fil-A Inc. "Fast Facts."

http://www.truettcathy.com/pdfs/CFAFastFacts.pdf .

City of Dayton. "Dayton Inventions."

http://www.daytonohio.gov/departments/pa/Pages/inventionlist.as

px.

Coca-Cola. http://www.coca-cola.com/en/index.html.

Collins, Jim. http://www.jimcollins.com/.

Dell, Michael S. "Michael S. Dell Keynote Address," The University of

Texas at Austin, 2003.

http://www.utexas.edu/commencement/2003/spring/speech.html.

Deloitte LLP. "2004 Deloitte Volunteer IMPACT Survey."

http://www.deloitte.com/view/en_US/us/About/Community-

Involvement/039d899a961fb110VgnVCM100000ba42f00aRCRD.

htm.

"DeWalt." Wikipedia, modified 1 October 2011.

http://en.wikipedia.org/wiki/DeWalt.

"Donald Trump." Wikiquote, modified 28 August 2011.

http://en.wikiquote.org/wiki/Donald_Trump.

Edison, Thomas.

http://www.brainyquote.com/quotes/quotes/t/thomasaed136875.ht

ml.

Entrepreneur.com. "Small Business Encyclopedia: Branding."

http://www.entrepreneur.com/encyclopedia/term/82248.html.

Ford, Henry. http://www.quotedb.com/quotes/2094.

Foreman, George. George Foreman Electric Grills.

http://www.georgeforemancooking.com/.

Frankl, Viktor E. *Man's Search for Meaning.* Pocket Books, 1946;1997.

Gitomer, Jeffery. http://www.gitomer.com/.

Grunder, Marty. Grunder Landscaping Company, Dayton, Ohio.

http://www.grunderlandscaping.com/.

Grunkemeyer, Mark. Buckeye Ecocare, Centerville, Ohio.

   http://www.buckeyeecocare.com/about/.

Hersey, Paul and Ken Blanchard. *Management of Organizational*

   *Behavior.* Prentice Hall, 2011.

Hobaica, Louis. Hobaica Services Inc., Phoenix, Arizona.

   http://www.hobaica.com/.

Holy Bible (King James, New King James, and New International

   Versions): Isaiah 40:31; Proverbs 19:20; and Exodus 18:13-26.

Humphrey, Albert. "Stakeholders Concept and SWOT Analysis," Stanford

   University, 1960-70.

Jobs, Steve. http://thinkexist.com/quotation/innovation-distinguishes-

   between-a-leader-and-a/392765.html.

Landry, Tom.

   http://humanresources.about.com/od/workrelationships/a/quotes_l

   eaders.htm.

Lim, Terence, PhD. "Social Impact, Business Benefits, and Investor

   Returns." Committee Encouraging Corporate Philanthropy, 2009.

   http://www.corporatephilanthropy.org/pdfs/resources/MVCP_repo

   rt_singles.pdf.

Lombardi, Vince. http://www.vincelombardi.com/.

Mathile, Clay. http://business.uc.edu/centers/goering/educational-

programs/business-institute.html.

Maxwell, John C. *The Maxwell Leadership Bible* (New King James

Version). Thomas Nelson Publishers, 2002.

Maxwell, John C. *Today Matters: 12 Daily Practices to Guarantee*

*Tomorrow's Success.* Center Street, 2004.

Mays, Benjamin.

http://www.morehouse.edu/about/chapel/mays_wisdom.html.

McAfee Foundation for Children and Youth, in Partnership with Dayton

Children's.

http://www.mcafeefoundation.com/makeadifference.htm.

McAfee, Greg. Greg McAfee Resources for HVAC Business Success. "A

Marketing Plan that Sets Your HVAC Business Apart."

http://www.1-800-air-repair.com/.

McAfee, Greg. Greg McAfee Resources for HVAC Business Success.

"Train Your HVAC Team with the Open Book Game of Business:

TOBGOB." http://www.tobgob.com/.

Minor and Brown PC, Attorneys and Counselors, Denver, Colorado.

http://www.minorbrown.com/about-us/.

Musico, Christopher. "Brand Lessons Learned from Mickey Mouse."

Destination CRM, 3 November 2009.

http://www.destinationcrm.com/Articles/CRM-News/Daily-

News/Brand-Lessons-Learned-from-Mickey-Mouse-57620.aspx.

Nike. http://www.nikebiz.com/?sitesrc=uslp.

"Quotes/Ronald Reagan." Wikipedia, modified 19 February 2008.

http://www.dkosopedia.com/wiki/Quotes/Ronald_Reagan.

Redenbacher, Orville. Orville Redenbacher's Gourmet Popping Corn.

http://www.orville.com/about-us/history.jsp.

Rogers, Will. http://www.leadershipnow.com/initiativequotes.html.

Rosenthal, Jim and Leo Mazzone. *Pitch Like a Pro: A Guide for Young

Pitchers and Their Coaches, Little League through High School.*

St. Martin's Griffin, 1999.

Rothschild, William E.

http://mysite.verizon.net/vzesz4a6/current/id317.html.

Schnatter, John. Papa John's.

http://company.papajohns.com/about/pj_story.shtm.

Seuss, Dr. *Happy Birthday To You!* Random House Children's Books, 2003.

Target Corporation. "Corporate Responsibility Report 2007." http://sites.target.com/images/corporate/about/responsibility_repor t/responsibility_report_social.pdf.

Thomas, Dave. Wendy's Restaurants. http://www.wendys.com/dave/.

Tucker, Preston. "The Tucker Automobile Club of America." http://www.tuckerclub.org/.

United States Congress. "American Recovery and Reinvestment Act of 2009." http://www.recovery.gov/About/Pages/The_Act.aspx.

United States Department of Commerce. Washington, DC. http://www.commerce.gov/.

VARtek K-12 Managed Technology, Dayton, Ohio. http://www.vartek.com/.

Wesley, John. http://quotationsbook.com/quote/27221/.

An award-winning entrepreneur, Greg McAfee has a passion for helping business owners take their businesses to new heights. In 1990, Greg started McAfee Heating and Air, his only capital a meager $274 and a well-used truck. Today, Greg runs one of the most successful HVAC companies in the Midwest and is called upon to share his expertise with other business owners all over the nation.

Greg McAfee exudes passion in all he does. As a proud veteran of the U.S. Marine Corps, Greg cares about people. Whether it's working with an HVAC contractor in Denver, Colorado, helping children through The McAfee Foundation, inspiring his team to take care of the customer, or following his own children's pursuits, Greg is devoted and committed. Nothing excites him more than talking to and encouraging small business owners who still have a passion for the business but are simply not happy with where they are. Greg loves to inspire others to chase their dreams at full force, just as he has in his own life.

Greg is still the working President of his company, consults and teaches other small business owners, and continues to dream big. He makes his home in Bellbrook, Ohio with his wife Naomi and their two children.